Wise Master Builder

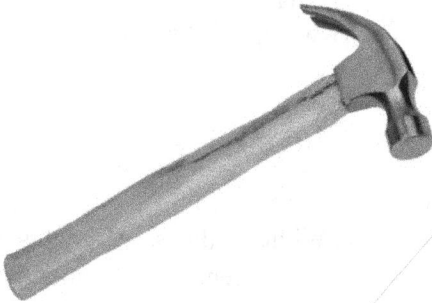

Dr. Willie Holmes

CLF Publishing, LLC.

9161 Sierra Ave, Ste. 203C
Fontana, CA 92335
www.clfpublishing.org

Cover Design by Senir Design. Contact information-info@senirdesign.com.

ISBN # 978-1-945102-13-4

Printed in the United States of America.

Dedications

In loving memory of my father and mother:
Paul and Elma Holmes
My wife Vanessa Holmes
My children Sherese, Willie Jr., Chloe, and Shaun
Mr. and Mrs. Kyle Colyar
The late Dr. Lavell Brown (best friend)
The Taylor Family
Emiel and Cecilia
Dr. Juanita Bynum
Mr. and Mrs. Cedeno
Mr. and Mrs. Bryant
And my administrative colleagues and board members.

I thank the authors, leaders, and research analysts who allowed me to use their life experiences to create such a book!

Everybody surrounded me with love, to accomplish this work of God's Kingdom.

Acknowledgements

Big shout to my God and Savior Jesus Christ

All past, present, and future staff members

G.N.A Family church members

G.N.A board members

Drs. Clyde and Yvonne Taylor (in-laws)

Walton family

Turner Family

Ater Family

Paul Family

Bryant Family

Pat Barber

Solomon Gabriel

Therese Kovach and Family

Luevonzae Stokes (United Goodwell Community Church)

Global Assemblies and Affiliates

Cannon Church of God in Christ and Church Family

Lisa Batshon

Mr. and Mrs. Hailu

Wanda Walker

Holmes Family

Kendra Esther

Cannan C.O.G.I.C.

The late Bob Dool

Rebeca Lopes

Dr. Laura Simpson

Ms. W. Walker

Mr. and Mrs. Given

Mr. and Mrs. Lary Robenson

Mr. and Mrs. Smoot

Miss Patricia Baber

Dr. Christine Clarke

Partners of Willie Holmes Ministries

Yoli Ornelas

Veynell Warren

Dr. Carolyn Singleton

Mr. and Mrs. Myles Tatum

Mr. and Mrs. Moore

Mr. Coffee

T.B.N Network

Matt and Laurie Crouch

Miss Fannie Lewis

Kings House

Debra & Shelly Ward

Arthur Taylor

Table of Contents

Chapter One
The Problem

Leadership in ministry is a compound technique where one will need to accomplish given tasks and objectives, and after accomplishing the tasks, the people he/she works with will remain as a team and not become disbanded. Leadership is also a management skill that one needs in order to manage the business aspect of ministry and/or to run a successful department in a church. Every successful ministry must have a leader. In order to be a leader, one must first be a great follower.

Statistics state that some pioneered churches close down after they reach their seventh year in operation. Reasons vary for the churches liquidation, and reasons also vary for other churches remaining in operation. However, it can be speculated that the liquidation may be a result of poor leadership. Thusly, if leadership was easy, almost everyone would be a leader. This demonstrates leadership is obviously not easy. Therefore, leadership can be viewed as an art.

Bass' theory of leadership states there are three basic ways to explain how people become leaders. The first two explain the leadership development for a small number of people. The first theory states some personality traits may lead people naturally into leadership roles. This is the Trait Theory. Second, a crisis or important event may cause a person to rise to the occasion, which brings out extraordinary leadership qualities in an ordinary person. This is the Great Events Theory. Third, people can choose to become leaders. People can learn leadership skills. This is the Transformational Leadership Theory. It is the most widely accepted theory today.

Being a pastor of a church means that one has certain leadership qualities, and God has entrusted that person to lead and preach to His people. The Bible teaches one philosophy of Christian Leadership. Christ Himself summarized and modeled it in Matthew 20. Principles of service and suffering form the basis of the leader's relationship to his/her subordinates, while the leader shows respect toward his/her ministerial colleagues as equals.

The Bible says in 1 Corinthians 3:10-13,
"According to the grace of God which is given unto me, as a wise masterbuilder, I have laid the foundation, and another buildeth thereon. But let every man take heed how he buildeth thereupon. For other foundation can no man lay than that is laid, which is Jesus Christ. Now if any man build upon this foundation gold, silver, precious stones, wood, hay, stubble; Every man's work shall be made manifest: for the day shall declare it, because it shall be revealed by fire; and the fire shall try every man's work of what sort it is."

In this reference tool, the solid foundation is Christ, and the foundation that is not firm is the enemy. A leader is illustrated as a builder, and the building that he/she builds is illustrated as the people (sheep) that he/she nourishes with the Word and by also loving them. God has given pastors the authority and the ability to lead His people, but the growth and success of the ministry depends on how the pastors or leaders build on that foundation and also how they duplicate themselves within the ministry. A builder must first determine the area where he/she plans on building (rural or suburb community) and must also know the vital things that make up a building. For example, he/she must determine the foundation on which the building will be built. What will hold up the ceilings and the walls? What will keep the rain out? What parts will go into making the building? How many different people are involved when that building goes up? What will determine the budget and how the funds will be disseminated to different contractors? One person makes the decisions, but it takes more than one person to complete the job. It takes unity.

The many attributes of leadership seem as though they can fall under one of two broad distinct categories: strategy and tactics. Strategic leadership gives the overall vision or end that needs to be accomplished. Meanwhile, tactical leadership deals with the details of achieving that vision or end. You need both, and each category defines a good leader in a different way. A war requires a general to oversee the entire military campaign. Meanwhile, commanders need to be on the field to guide the troops. Likewise, a CEO may create and execute an excellent strategy to guide a corporation to profitability and market dominance. However, tactical leaders are needed to manage sales teams, maintain efficient operations, and develop innovative products.

It will be particularly interesting to see whether leaders in the two categories (i.e. strategy and tactics) need to share leadership attributes at all and how easy it would be for them to switch from role to role; certainly, everyone has his/her own needs, but how necessary is it to actually have those lauded "transferable" skills?

Statement of the Problem

A concern in ministry is that leaders (pastors) that have the ability to start off in ministry with the right motive, right resources, and the right people (sheep), whether considering a large church with multiple staff and a well-developed pastoral department or a single staff church ended up going in a different direction. For instance, I started off in ministry with the right intent, but later ended up incarcerated and hurting others. But, bless the Lord, through God's redemption and my enlightenment of the tools, I was able to get back on track. Many times the success of a ministry is predicated on how a leader duplicates him/herself within his/her members or how he/she trains his/her staff. These members could be from different backgrounds, specifically ethnicity, upbringing, and belief.

This book is to be used to identify the strengths and weaknesses of a builder and what it takes to be a successful leader who serves as a 'servant'. Everybody has a dream, but not everyone accomplishes that dream for various reasons. The Bible says that wisdom is the principal thing, meaning that it is vital in all areas of ministry.

Everybody will not be a part of your dream. Some people come across your path to assist a leader to move from point A to point B, and some people will be with a leader until the accomplishment of that given dream.

Purpose and Objective of Study

This reference tool takes a look at the leadership's personality traits in ministry. Bass' theory of leadership will be used in this reference tool as explained in the introduction to show how people can become leaders and how to identify a leader within a group of people. Dr. Taylor Hartman identifies four primary personality profiles using colors to describe them: red, blue, yellow and white. This personality test, which I have personally used with my staff, will be used to show one's strengths, how to transform weaknesses, and also how to enhance one's business performance.

Red personalities are logical, direct, determined, resourceful and very driven. They share a strong quest for power. They want to be in control. Reds tend to be good, productive leaders who are also selfish and insensitive to the needs of others.

Blue personalities are reliable, loyal, emotional and controlling. They tend to be perfectionists and worry a lot; they thrive on relationships. Blues want to love and be loved by others. Their core motive is intimacy. They tend to be nurturing and altruistic but also perfectionistic and controlling.

Yellow personalities are optimistic, happy, adventurous

and spontaneous. Yellows want life to be fun and exciting. They tend to be the life of the party and easy-going, but also irresponsible and emotionally shallow. Educational pursuits take a back seat to friends and fun.

White personalities are reflective, peaceful, adaptable and independent. They tend to be smart, reclusive "thinkers" who do not demand praise or special recognition. Whites want harmony, peace, and for everyone to just get along. They tend to be amiable and diplomatic. They also tend to be lazy and bottle up grievances until they explode.

Method and Procedure

A. *Method*

This reference tool' focus is on teaching and training for the purpose of developing leaders. Many times in the development stages, 'leaders in the making' tend to get discouraged because of disappointment. One principle that must be enforced is, *'In order to be a leader, you must first become a servant.'* The ministers in churches should, when teaching leaders, make sure they emphasize the importance of confessing God's Word daily, from the Bible, relating to whatever challenges they have. For example, a leader who easily gets discouraged or feels like he/she is a failure can use the scripture below,

"I can do all things through Christ who strengthens me."
Philippians 4:18

Having a strong prayer life is very essential. One must

also emphasize that the staff is not there for that leader but for God. They must understand that they are not serving man but God, who is the rewarder of them that diligently seek Him (Hebrews 11:6). If a minister builds strong people, he/she will in turn build a strong church. One thing I have learned personally is that one cannot change a person, but God can. An individual has to be willing to change and also be willing to make mistakes and make room for mistakes. In training the leaders, this will involve implementation of any given tasks within the group. A minister should start off with small assignments and observe how that leader handles that assignment. In this implementation, Dr. Taylor Hartman's personality test may be used. Another essential tool in the training process is communication. One may communicate directly to a person or by means of a memorandum.

B. *Procedure*

Below are the steps a minister may use for the procedure:

1. Monitor the staff on a weekly or bi-weekly basis.
2. Have standard meetings and roundtable discussions on a routine basis to determine the outcome.
3. Have a grading or point system.
4. Attendance at staff meetings when things are offered.
5. Listen and reward your staff for doing a great job. This will keep them encouraged.
6. Allow them to share their hearts, and as their example, listen to what they have to say.
7. Conference call
8. Social Media

Scope of the Study

This reference tool includes an overview of Bass' Theory of Leadership, the four types of leaders using Dr. Taylor Hartman's method of personality profiles (reds, blues, yellows, and whites), and specific therapeutic tools that can be used to relieve stress from one's staff. Sometimes, a minister sees the potential in an individual and knows that he/she has the leadership qualities or has the potential to work with a group, but the individual's attitude can be unpleasant. Therefore, a minister must know how to love that person, get him/her involved, and teach, train and develop him/her. In this reference tool, a builder is likened to a minister, the staff members are the builders, and the foundation is the Word of God.

Summary and Overview

This book includes five chapters. **Chapter One** starts the book with an introduction to the subject, states the problem in churches today with leadership, and highlights the objective of this reference tool. **Chapter Two** will highlight and clarify the theories mentioned in Chapter One. **Chapter Three** analyzes the main objective and discusses the Dr. Taylor Hartman's method of personality profiles in detail. **Chapter Four** discusses the theology of a servant leadership. **Chapter Five** concludes and summarizes the entire book.

Chapter Two
Literature Review

Overview of the Topic

This review of literature will focus on A) training upcoming international leaders from different backgrounds, upbringings, social classes, and ethnicities. B) Motivation as they relate to workplace productivity, and the overall success of all departments within a ministry. C) Identifying potentials (strength and weakness of a leader. D) Crisis prevention by using Dr. Taylor Hartman's personality profiles.

Scope and Limitations of this Review

The literature in this review is established biblically. It focuses on the dimensions of leadership, leaders' and members' behaviors, and how leadership is measured and attributed by others. Special emphasis is placed upon the effect of members' behaviors in a ministry. Both historic and contemporary writings were reviewed with extra attention given to those authors who have gained popular acceptance or who have been widely replicated. This review is limited to the most validated theories and accepted principles.

Organization of the Literature Review

The discussion portion of this review describes a leader who is biblically likened to a wise master builder, through historical and contemporary studies of leadership and member's behavior. It centers on how leader's actions are classified and how both followers and higher-level leaders attribute leadership qualities and traits to the person in charge. Dr. Taylor Hartman's profiles the fourteen traits of good leadership, dream builders and dream killers. Further, the review surveyed the roles of leaders in attaining productive results within departments in a ministry. This chapter discusses the motivational factors, which influence member's productivity and organizational success. Finally, a summary section ties together the philosophies, concepts, evidence, theories and practices discussed in this review.

Discussion
Wise Master Builder
The Bible says in Acts 6:3 (KJV):
"Wherefore, brethren, look ye out among you seven men of honest report, full of the Holy Ghost and wisdom, whom we may appoint over this business."

A minister must always be careful to choose leaders who understand they are in ministry to please God and not man, and he/she must also make sure that the position he/she is entrusting them with they are able to work in and handle pressure without experiencing 'ministry burn out.' It is also critical to distinguish between the skill of performance and the skill of leading performance. For example, a children's ministry worker that is not good with infants cannot be a department head of the Children's Ministry.

In reference to the above scripture, Matthew Henry's Commentary notes that preaching the gospel is the best work and is the most proper and needful work that a minister can be employed in, and that he/she must give him/herself wholly to it (1 Tim. 4:15). In doing so, he/she must not entangle him/herself in the affairs of this life (2 Tim. 2:4), no, not in the outward business of the house of God (Neh. 11:16).

Note- Those that are employed in any office in the church ought to be men of honest report, of a blameless, nay, of an admirable character, which is requisite not only to the credit of their office, but to the discharge of it. Secondly, they must be full of the Holy Ghost, must be filled with those gifts and graces of the Holy Ghost, which were necessary to the right management of this trust. They must not only be honest men, but they must be men of ability and men of courage, such as were to be made judges in Israel (Ex. 18:21), able men, fearing God; men of truth, and hating covetousness; and hereby appearing to be full of the Holy Ghost. Thirdly, they must be full of wisdom. It was not enough that they were honest, good men, but they must also be discreet, judicious men, that could not be imposed upon, and would order things for the best, and with consideration: full of the Holy Ghost, and wisdom, that is, of the Holy Ghost as a Spirit of wisdom. We find the word of wisdom given by the Spirit, as distinct form the word of knowledge by the same Spirit, (1 Cor. 12:8).

The scripture also says in Ephesians 4:11 (KJV):
"And he gave some, apostles; and some, prophets; and some, evangelists; and some, pastors and teachers; For the perfecting of the saints, for the work of the ministry, for the edifying of the body of Christ."

Appointing leadership over various departments will require wisdom. Not everyone is called to the children's department, nor is everyone called to the pastoral ministry. A minister should identify what the interests of the leaders are and if they are willing to work. In Chapter One, it was mentioned that a person can have the potential and yet have an unpleasant attitude. Your attitude will determine your altitude. In the Bible, David had the right attitude even though Saul wanted to kill him. Even though David ran away to protect himself, he still went back to his assignment because he was not trying to please man but God, and also, his motive was right towards Saul and towards God.

The importance of leadership in everyday life is manifest in the vast number of books, articles and other writings available today. In considering the development of leadership, we have to examine two different courses of life history:

1. Development through socialization, which prepares the individual to guide institutions and to maintain the

existing balance of social relations, and

2. Development through personal mastery, which impels an individual to struggle for psychological and social change.

3. Society produces its managerial talent through the first line of development.

4. Leaders emerge through the second.

The leader uses vision, encouragement and example to help keep the members of an organization learning. Each of these qualities is further defined by Handy in the following list.

1. Vision. No one will go through the arduous task of learning unless there is vision. Most people want to share in a task that is bigger than themselves. They want a purpose in life beyond themselves, something real not just rhetoric. Visions must be earthed in reality. Standards are the currency of vision. But standards need compare-sons, one of the benefits of competition. Competition sets standards.

2. Learning needs constant encouragement, including the satisfaction of having learned something. Learning feeds on itself. Measuring results can help, because progress is then made visible. Recognition helps even more.

3. Ultimately, personal examples matter most in keeping the wheel moving. The leader who says, "Learning is good for you, but I don't need it," will have few followers.

We would rather have a leader who is seen to be open-minded, questions him/herself and others, searches for ideas, is obsessed with truth and betterment, is ready to take risks, listens to criticism and advice, and has a purpose beyond him/herself combined with an awareness that he/she cannot do it on his/her own. Give that leader self-confidence and a sense of humour, and most would be happy to follow his/her example (4).

After years of highly focused research, Bennis found four key elements of effective leadership. His findings reinforce the conclusions of much of the leadership research to date.

Bennis uses the concept of "leadership strategies."

1. Attention through vision. The leader has an agenda, an unparalleled concern with outcome.

2. Meaning through communication. All organizations depend on the existence of shared meanings and interpretations of reality, which facilitate coordinated action. An essential factor in leadership is the capacity to influence and organize meaning for the members of the organization.

3. Trust through positioning. To achieve trust, the leader must be the epitome not only of clarity, but of constancy and reliability. Establishing organizational integrity and "staying the course" are key elements of this strategy.

4. The deployment of self through positive self-regard and the Wallenda factor. Leadership is a highly personal activity. (1) The leader must recognize strengths and compensate for weaknesses, nurture skills with discipline, and discern the fit between one's strengths and the needs of the

organization. (2) Effective leaders do not think about failure. They do not even use the word. When Karl Wallenda (famed tightrope walker) focused on not falling, he was doomed to fall. Leaders, who succeed, focus on success, rather than thinking about the consequences of failure (26-70). The first two of Bennis' strategies incorporate the concept of "initiation of structure" or task orientation, while strategy Number 3 reflects the idea of consideration. The fourth strategy reinforces the idea of personal competence and confidence. The words indicate a strong internal focus of control in such leaders.

These studies provide a clear picture of the effective leader: one who has a vision and is able to communicate it well to his/her followers; a person who actively listens to subordinates, seeks their opinions, cares about them and earns their trust; a highly visible individual, who believes he/she controls outcomes; one who helps followers to succeed through guidance and teaching; a person who knows what must be done and arranges the situation to get results.

Such leadership traits and actions are identified throughout the literature. In fact, it is difficult to find dissenting views on these conclusions. Observing organizations over the past forty years, I have come to the conclusion that seldom does a single person demonstrate all of the traits together. Frequently, several people combine to bring all the traits to bear upon the organization. Working in concert, a team of leaders compliments each other to achieve the desired results.

The sixteen dimensions used by the Army in its Leadership Assessment Program (LAP) are similar to the skills listed by other leadership researchers, both military and civilian. The LAP dimensions are listed below.

1. Oral Communication. The ability to express oneself effectively in individual or group situations, including gestures and other nonverbal communication.

2. Oral Presentation. The ability to present concepts, information, or tasks to an individual or group when given time for preparation; includes gestures and other nonverbal communication.

3. Written Communication. The skill required to express ideas clearly, in writing, using good grammatical form.

4. Initiative. The discipline that requires attempting to influence events and achieve goals beyond those called for; originating action; self-starting rather than passive acceptance.

5. Sensitivity. Those actions that indicate a consideration for the feeling and needs of others.

6. Influence. The art of using appropriate interpersonal styles and methods in guiding subordinates, peers, supervisors, or groups toward task accomplishment.

7. Delegation. The ability to use the talents of subordinates effectively: the allocation of decision-making and other responsibilities to subordinates.

8. Administrative Control. The ability to establish procedures for coordinating actions and activities of subordinates, and fulfilling duty requirements and responsibilities; to monitor the progress and results of delegated assignments.

9. Problem Analysis. The skill to recognize and define a problem, relate problem data from different sources, and determine possible problem causes and solutions.
10. Judgment. The ability to develop alternative courses of action and make decisions based on logical assumptions that reflect experience and factual information.
11. Planning and Organizing. The ability to establish a course of action for self or others toward a specific goal; planning proper assignments of personnel and appropriate allocation of resources.
12. Decisiveness. The readiness to make decisions, render judgments, take action, or commit oneself.
13. Physical Stamina. The ability to accomplish required tasks under conditions of physical, mental and emotional stress. To lead by example and set the pace in physical tasks while in a leadership position and to maintain the pace set by the group in physical activity while a follower.
14. Technical/Tactical Competence. A level of understanding and ability to use technical and tactical proficiency to accomplish tasks to specified standards; includes demonstrated understanding of technical knowledge and skills.
15. Mission Accomplishment. The ability to complete individual and unit assigned tasks according to specified standards and within time allotments.
16. Followership. Willing and wholehearted cooperation in the accomplishment of missions. Respect for authority and subordination of personal preferences. Doing one's best in discharging designated responsibilities (Leadership 2-6 to 2-15).

Attaining Productive Results in a Ministry

A. *14 Traits of Good Leadership*

A minister may use the following 14 traits of good leadership, which are used in colleges, universities and the Armed Forces Officer Training Programs, to determine the qualities of the leaders in the group as well as for training:

01. <u>Bearing</u> is a good professional appearance and conduct.
02. <u>Courage</u> is being calm and firm in the face of danger and criticism.
03. <u>Decisiveness</u> is the ability to make decisions promptly.
04. <u>Dependability</u> is the certainty of proper performance of job and duty.
05. <u>Endurance</u> in both mental and physical stamina.
06. <u>Enthusiasm</u> is the display of sincere interest and zeal.
07. <u>Initiative</u> is the ability to take actions in the absence of orders.
08. <u>Integrity</u> is truthfulness and honesty.
09. <u>Judgment</u> assessed on the weight of facts, solutions and alternatives.
10. <u>Justice</u> is the impartiality in giving rewards and punishments.
11. <u>Knowledge</u> is knowing your job, your group members and yourself.
12. <u>Loyalty</u> is faithfulness to the group, and your minister.
13. <u>Tact</u> is the ability to deal with others respectfully.
14. <u>Unselfishness</u> is placing others before yourself.

B. *Crisis Prevention*
Below is Dr. Taylor Hartman's personality profile comparing personality types.

RED	BLUE	YELLOW	WHITE
Personalities are logical, direct, determined, resourceful, and very driven. They are strong and quest for power. They want to be in control. Reds tend to be good, productive leaders that are also selfish and insensitive to the needs of others.	*Blue personalities are reliable, loyal, emotional and controlling. They tend to be perfectionists and worry a lot; they thrive on relationships. Blues want to love and be loved by others, their core motive being intimacy. They tend to be nurturing and altruistic but also perfectionistic and controlling.*	*Yellow personalities are optimistic, happy, adventurous and spontaneous. Yellows want life to be fun and exciting. They tend to be the life of the party and easy-going, but also irresponsible and emotionally shallow. Educational pursuits are secondary to friends and fun.*	*White personalities are reflective, peaceful, adaptable and independent. They tend to be smart, reclusive "thinkers" who do not demand praise or special recognition. Whites want harmony and peace, and for everyone to just get along. They tend to be amiable and diplomatic. They also tend to be lazy and bottle up grievances until they explode.*

Before you choose your group, you must identify personalities first. Do not mix a group with same personalities. Difference is good, and it creates balance. Make sure you have one of each: red, yellow, blue and white. This will prevent any crisis in your group. Try to meet with your group every often and encourage them to be honest with you, so you can build unity amongst them. Communicate, communicate, communicate.

Face-to-face meetings between leaders and employees are a hallmark of world-class organizations. Continuous, open communication throughout the organization is a must. Especially important are the four key business processes: strategy development, planning, deployment and business prioritization. Introduce fun things and have moments of laughter. Do not allow your group to be bored. Boredom is the killer to your dream. Do not allow situations and old mental stumbling blocks to kill your dream! Below is a list of dream builders and killers that your group can evaluate themselves by periodically:

a) Avoid the not-invented-here syndrome. It isn't necessary to reinvent the wheel. Use what other companies have done: Build upon it.

b) Make leaders students first. All managers, senior, middle and front line need to experience training on quality topics before they can be expected to lead effectively.

c) Leaders must know how to systematically follow the steps to quality. Don't expect a magic bullet. The Baldrige Award criteria are a guide. Using it once is not enough. The quality process is ongoing: It never ends.

d) Just do it! Avoid the temptation to plan to plan. Allocate resources to achieve the quality goals, then get on with the actions to reach those goals (Brennan 54-58). Blazey reinforces the above tenets by suggesting that managers lead by example. He notes that the leader must be a visionary who helps to focus the energies of the company on satisfying its customers. Communication with the work force is essential, as is gaining the cooperation of the front line people in the continuous improvement effort. He strongly states the connection between organizational success and effective leadership.

Leadership Success

"Leadership focuses on the creation of a common vision... George Weathersby	"Management is the design of work...it's about controlling..." George Weathersby

The Paradoxical Commandments: Kent M. Keith

1. People are illogical, unreasonable, and self-centered. Love them anyway.
2. If you do well, people will accuse you of selfish ulterior motives. Do well anyway.
3. If you are successful, you will win false friends and true enemies. Succeed anyway.
4. The good you do today will be forgotten tomorrow. Do well anyway.
5. Honesty and frankness make you vulnerable. Be honest and frank anyway.

6. The biggest men and women with biggest ideas can be shot down by the smallest men and women with the smallest minds. Think big anyway.
7. People favor underdogs but follow only top dogs. Fight for a few underdogs anyway.
8. What you spend years building may be destroyed overnight. Build anyway.
9. People really need help but may attack you if you do help them. Help people anyway.
10. Give the world the best you have, and you'll get kicked in the teeth. Give the world the best you have anyway.

The 7 Habits of Highly Effective People

1. Be Proactive
2. Begin with the End in Mind
3. Put First Things First
4. Think Win-Win
5. Seek First to Understand, Then to be Understood
6. Synergize- It's the fruit of respecting, valuing and even celebrating one another's differences. It's about solving problems, seizing opportunities, and working out differences. A synergistic team is a complementary team- where the team is organized so that the strengths of some compensate for the weaknesses of others.
7. Sharpen the Saw- sharpening the saw is about constantly renewing ourselves in the four basic areas of life: physical, social/emotional, mental and spiritual. It's the habit that increases our capacity to live all other habits of effectiveness.

In *Thriving on Chaos*, Peters (x) devotes ten chapters to behavioral prescriptions for leadership success. Because of the depth of his analysis, his ten actions are listed below together with descriptive explanations.

1. Master paradox. The core paradox, then, that all leaders at all levels must contend with is fostering internal stability in order to encourage the pursuit of constant change.

2. Develop an inspiring vision. The vision must provide stability-it inspires the confidence necessary to induce constant risk-taking in pursuit of its execution/perfection/expansion.

3. Manage by example. So it boils down to this: Want to call attention to your new quality program? There is only one way that counts with the organization's members: Spend time on it-lots of time.

4. Practice visible management. The most effective leaders, from Mohandas Gandhi to Sam Walton of Wal-Mart, have always led from the front line, where the action is.

5. Pay attention! (More Listening). Today's successful leaders will work diligently to engage others in their cause. Oddly enough, the best way, by far, to engage others is by listening-seriously listening-to them.

6. Defer to the front line. Success in today's environment will come when those on the front line are honored as heroes and empowered to act-period. A prime leadership task is to ensure that honor goes to the line and those who support it most vigorously.

7. Delegate. We must learn to let go, or suffer the consequences of unacceptably slow action- taking the plain fact is that nine out of ten managers haven't delegated enough.

8. Pursue "horizontal" management by bashing bureaucracy. We must pursue fast-paced action at all costs, and therefore: vigorously and gleefully, with all hands participating, take the lead in destroying the trappings of bureaucracy.
9. Evaluate everyone on his/her love of change. Change must become the norm, not cause for alarm. To up the odds for survival, leaders at all levels must become obsessive about change.
10. Create a sense of urgency. Since our foremost need is to change more, at a faster pace, we must: induce a sense of urgency and hustle throughout the organization; and seek to minimize potentially paralyzing fears, despite the uncertainty, which makes fearfulness legitimate (472-568).

Dream Builders and Dream Killers

What is a "vision"? A "vision" is an attainable dream. It involves two aspects:

1. A dream
2. A workable plan.

This means a goal of great value, difficult to attain, requiring long-term investment of time and personnel. Both must exist to qualify as "vision." A plan without a dream lacks the momentum to attract the necessary leaders to make it work. A dream without a plan is merely visionary and never gets off the ground.

The Protestant Reformation was the result of the vision of several men like Luther, Calvin and Knox. It was a goal of immense value, costing many lives over three generations. The religious freedom and prosperity many countries enjoy today is the direct result of that vision.

In the political domain, the Latin American revolution under Simon Bolivar was the result of a vision. Bolivar dreamed of the liberation of an entire continent. It was costly and required a lifetime investment of resources, a continent was worth it.

A vision need not be as ambitious as the above examples. Every successful church or Christian organization was started by a person with the vision to see it happen.

A Vision Without a Plan is Merely Visionary

Listening to a visionary may be entertaining, but so are movies. Eloquence does not equal vision, either. Certain articulate and intelligent people discourse eloquently about what needs to be done. They seem more adept at analyzing the deficiencies of others than creating workable plans. Though they appear knowledgeable and confident, one never quite grasps exactly what they are saying. It is like catching smoke. (Politicians are often like that.) These are visionaries at best and leaders, not at all...wind-bags to be ignored.

A Dream and a Plan are Not Quite Enough

Some may have a dream and a plan and still not be leaders. A third element must enter in... the personal drive and commitment to implement it. Without this, all they will be doing is trying to persuade others to do the work.

A dream and a plan without 'drive' is like a sports car with a driver who won't turn the key to start the engine.

A. *Elements of a Sensible Vision*

   1. Simplicity. You must be able to explain your vision in a few seconds. Otherwise, it is too complex. People need to understand it to support it. Your promotional literature should project the vision in the first line or two. Slogans and acronyms help. If you can come up with a slogan, this will help people grasp the idea.

   2. Difficult but not impossible. If it were easy, somebody would have already done it. If the goal is attainable and desirable, but has not been done, it is either because nobody believes it is possible or no one has the drive to attempt it.

To accomplish a vision, it takes a person who can distinguish between impossible and difficult. The ability to take what others see as impossible and evolve a plan for doing it is the difference between a Christian worker and a Christian leader.

Characteristics of a Godly Vision

  A. *It Must Advance the Kingdom of God, Not Your Own Self-Esteem.* How does your vision advance the Kingdom of God and produce holy people? Remember, God's goal is to create a holy people for His Kingdom and glorify His name this way. Anything we do must fit into this goal or our idea did not come from God. Some have built their own empires as monuments to themselves in the name of God's Kingdom. Others have a strong psychological need to affirm their own self-worth. Beware of motives.

B. *It Must be Based on a Personal Call from God.* Just because it is a good idea does not necessarily mean it is God's call for us to accomplish it. David had a great idea for building a temple to honor God. Nathan the prophet informed him that God was pleased with the idea, but it was Solomon who was called do it. Although the Bible teaches only one philosophy of Christian leadership, leadership styles may differ, depending on temperaments and circumstances. Some are pioneers, others managers or maintenance people, while still others are computer engineers, singers, song writers, actors. A leader is partly characterized by having the initial vision. A vision is an attainable and valuable dream, which comes from God.

10 Dream Killers

Do you...

...ignore your inner voice and desire?

...struggle to say what you really want?

...strive to meet others' expectations of you?

...allow someone else's dream to become your priority?

...dwell on your perceived inadequacies?

...hide your strengths for fear of being different?

...hesitate to leave the familiarity of your disillusionment?

...run from the responsibilities of your success?

...fear to make mistakes?

...believe it is too late to change or try new things?

Dream Builders

Do you...

> ...desire success, prosperity, and joy?
> ...believe in yourself and your personal power?
> ...visualize your dream and name aloud?
> ...think big and plan for greatness?
> ...disregard the naysayers?
> ...build upon your strengths and talents?
> ...attract people who can help you build your dream?
> ... recognize that mistakes are an important aspect of learning?
> ...nurture your body, mind and spirit?
> ...follow your passion?

Refrain from partiality and showing favoritism. That will create a spirit of jealousy, which will lead to gossip and later on division. A minister must always watch out for 'cliques' and do not be afraid to call them out.

Always tell your members how great they are and reward them after doing a great job. Do not allow for them to be too familiar with you because then there will be no respect for you. Teach your group how not to have a spirit of offense, nor 'wear their emotions on their sleeves', thus being easily offended by anything. Do not allow them to measure their success against someone else's in the group. This will decrease their self-esteem. Let your group know that they are dreamers. The poorest person is not the one without a nickel in his/her pocket, but it is the person without a dream. A person without a dream believes only in what is seen, only what is immediate, only what one can put his/her hands on. This person may be a student, a truck driver, a banker, a college president, a clerk or a junk dealer. The occupation doesn't matter. One of life's greatest tragedies is a person with a 10-by-12 capacity and a two-by-four soul(Hildebrand).

It is like a prisoner that has confined him/herself to a 6-by-8 cell when he/she could be living on earth with no bars attached. There is great difference in man-made dreams and God-given dreams. Man-made dreams will not stand the test of time and difficulties. A person without a God-given dream lacks depth and vision. Too many have planned all their lives to retire and failed to live that long. Only God can give you a worthwhile vision for your life. Through a study of God's Word, you can develop a worthwhile vision for your life. A person without a God-given dream is like a great ship made for the mighty ocean but trying to navigate in a millpond. This person has no far port to reach, no lifting horizon, and no precious cargo to carry. Her/his hours are absorbed in routine and petty tyrannies. It is a small wonder if this person gets dissatisfied, quarrelsome and 'fed up.' Watch out for the negatively minded in your dream team.

Maguire and Williford provide practical advice to leaders who wish to "walk the talk." His list of twelve keys complement the previous prescriptions, while adding renewed focus on communication, direction and action. He says of the following list: "These 12 guidelines for walking the talk can spell the difference between success and failure for a continuous improvement program" (21).

1. Say what you are going to do in simple, concise terms.
2. Do what you say you are going to do.
3. Convince leaders to become champions.
4. Tell stories to connect employees to what matters in their terms.
5. Put every improvement idea to the 'what matters' test.
6. Ask only for feedback you intend to act upon.
7. Set boundaries; then, get out of the way.
8. Fight scope creep and get closure.
9. Recognize and reward closure.
10. Make failure okay-for the right reasons.
11. Make skeptics part of the solution.
12. Acknowledge the past and learn from it (21).

The literature abounds with examples and principles of leadership in action. Underlying much of the discussion is the assumption that leaders are essential to the organization. In fact, a number of writers consider effective leadership to be the single most important factor influencing organizational success and worker productivity. The following quotations provide an indication of the perceived importance of leadership. How leaders develop and live a new model of leadership is and will be the most critical success factor for most every business (Belasco & Stayer 16). Without effective leadership at all levels in private and public organizations, it is difficult to sustain profitability, productivity, quality, and good customer service

(Dubrin xvii). If it [leadership] isn't widespread and working effectively, then the quality management scheme in that company simply is not working--no matter how much the company is dutifully 'filling the squares' to impress both themselves and the evaluators (Creech & Herrington 297-298).

Most of us unconsciously learned leadership at age seven, when we first observed leadership in Sunday school or with Brownies or Cub Scouts. There's that person (leader) who walks into the room, things are going moderately well, but the whole place clams up and goes stiff. Then, there's that other person (leader) who walks in, and even if things are going badly, you feel just a little bit better. There's a little more buzz in the air, just because of his or her presence (Peters: Seminar 204). Associated with almost every excellent company is a strong leader (or two) who seemed to have had a lot to do with making the company excellent in the first place (Peters & Waterman 26).

Leadership is the very heart and soul of business management. In my mind, the quality of leadership is the single most important ingredient in the recipe for business success (Geneen & Bowers 133). Although mediocre companies can be quite well managed, it's only leadership that can transform such companies into great organizations (Secretan 122). One final comment on the effects of leader behavior emphasizes one of the key features noted by most researchers concerning important attributes of leaders: Effective leaders listen to their subordinates, carefully. Anthony Jay indicate the impact on organizations of leaders who do not actively listen: "One of the prime causes of fury that crops up again and again in large organizations is leadership that do not listen."

Other contemporary writers suggest specific processes and activities are key to success. The variety of lists highlighted below provides a sense of these prescriptions. One of the most influential recent management gurus was W. Edwards Deming, known to many as the father of quality management. He was adamant that to be successful in the long term, an organization must follow his fourteen points as described by Walton and Deming in The Deming Management Method (vii-viii).

1. Create constancy of purpose for the improvement of product and service.
2. Adopt the new philosophy.
3. Cease dependence on mass inspection.
4. End the practice of awarding business on price tag alone.
5. Improve constantly and forever the system of production and service.
6. Institute training and retraining.
7. Institute leadership.
8. Drive out fear.
9. Break down barriers between staff areas.
10. Eliminate slogans, exhortations, and targets for the workforce.
11. Eliminate numerical quotas.
12. Remove barriers to pride of workmanship.
13. Institute a vigorous program of education and retraining.
14. Take action to accomplish the transformation.

Furthermore, in their best-selling book, *In Search of Excellence*, Peters and Waterman list and defend "eight basic principles to stay on top of the heap" (i).

1. A bias for action.
2. Staying close to the customer.
3. Autonomy and entrepreneurship.
4. Productivity through people.
5. Hands-on, value driven.
6. Stick to the knitting.
7. Simple form, lean staff.
8. Simultaneous loose-tight properties.

In the book he calls a "Handbook for a Management Revolution," *Thriving On Chaos*, Tom Peters provides forty-seven prescriptions for "a world turned upside down" (i-ii). He categorizes his tenets into five major categories.

1. Creating total customer responsiveness.
2. Pursuing fast-paced innovation.
3. Achieving flexibility by empowering people.
4. Learning to love change: a new view of leadership at all levels.
5. Building systems for a world turned upside down.

Secretan describes his own approach to organizational success in terms of seven key steps. He elaborates on these steps in his book, *Managerial Moxie*. His steps are remarkable in their similarity to the practices advocated by Deming, Walton, Peters and Waterman.

1. Develop a crystal clear sense of purpose in an organization.

2. Establish the appropriate climate in which success can happen.
3. Motivate the average employee to turn in an uncommon performance.
4. Hire superstars who create an organization-wide "can do" attitude.
5. Decentralize decision-making and diffuse authority through empowerment.
6. Energize an organization with a customer first philosophy.
7. Steer an organization through the judicious use of a few critical controls (478).

Another highly successful executive, Ken Iverson of Nucor Steel, expresses similar points of view concerning how to manage successfully. He makes five points:

- Destroy hierarchy: management exists to help workers do their jobs.
- You need trust to operate efficiently.
- Give workers a stake in the success of the business.
- Centralization vs. decentralization is not the issue-decisiveness is.
- Don't overlook the virtues of smallness (*The Art* 6).

In *Wisdom of Teams*, Katzenbach and Smith list the six things they feel are essential to good team leadership.
1. Keep the purpose, goals, and approach relevant and meaningful.
2. Build commitment and confidence.
3. Strengthen the mix and level of skills.

4. Manage relationships with outsiders, including removing obstacles.
5. Create opportunities for others.
6. Do real work (139-144).

Donald Weiss, author of the book, *Secrets of the Wild Goose*, suggests five ways the leader can support people in teams.
1. Model team behavior.
2. Provide "as-needed, real-time" training.
3. Track team performance.
4. Support guerilla teams (skunkworks).
5. Listen carefully to others. Use what you learn as a springboard to action (4-5).

In their book, Heroz and Cox list several "spells" to be cast by the leader or other influential person in the organization. The first set of spells direct how one should behave toward others in the workplace.
1. Maintain or enhance self-esteem.
2. Listen and respond with empathy.
3. Ask for and encourage involvement.

The next spell describes actions used to solve problems and implement solutions.
1. Assess Situation and Define Problem.
2. Determine Causes.
3. Target Solutions and Develop Ideas.
4. Implement Ideas.

5. Make it an Ongoing Process.

Finally, the authors list five actions essential to effective interaction.
1. Open with what is to be accomplished and why it is important.
2. Clarify the details.
3. Develop ideas.
4. Agree on actions.
5. Close with review decisions and set appropriate follow-up (194-196).

In a more procedural vein, Wilkins suggests five ways to build a quality business in his book, *The Quality Empowered Business.*
1. Assess current business opportunities.
2. Establish a cultural foundation.
3. Create an information network.
4. Streamline the delivery system.
5. Build partnerships with circle-4 customers (vi).

Martin Jones describes a four-step strategy for growing entrepreneurial organizations.
1. Decentralize decision-making.
2. Develop a high tolerance for risk.
3. Determine, develop and use people assets.
4. Make the financial function commercially oriented and user-friendly (2).

As one might expect, the procedural lists each contain elements of interpersonal dealings as well as managerial actions, including planning, organizing, directing and controlling. Also, each prescription for success assumes someone in a leadership role to implement and guide the steps. None of the management writers expects anything to happen without the involvement of a dedicated, action-oriented leader associated with a willing team of workers. In fact, each process includes steps through which the leader is expected to motivate and energize his/her followers. The role and effects of such motivation are discussed below.

Good leaders remember to recognize and motivate employees. Great leaders do it every day. Here are some proven methods for making sure that praising your team members becomes part of your daily routine.

- Make employees a part of your daily "to do" list. Cross their names off as you praise them.
- Use voice mail. Leave employees voice messages praising them for a job well done.
- Write notes at the end of the day. Take a minute to write thank-you notes to any employee who made a difference that day.
- At the beginning of the day, put five coins in your pocket. Then, during the day, each time you praise an employee, transfer a coin to the other pocket (1). A very successful Chief Executive Officer, Bill Marriott, of Marriott Hotels echoes the thoughts of many of his contemporaries. Motivate employees, train them, care about them, and make winners of

them. At Marriott, we know that if we treat our employees correctly, they'll treat the customers correctly. And if the customers are treated right, they'll come back (9). An unnamed consultant noted in Positive Leadership emphasizes how employee perceptions can affect motivational factors in the work place. "The more I work with organizations, the more I am convinced that it all comes down to how people-both employees and customers-perceive the way they are treated by the organization and its management" (5). Nelson notes: "Few concepts are as solidly founded as the idea that positive reinforcement- rewarding behavior you want repeated-works. In fact, in today's business climate, rewards and recognition have become more important than ever ..." (xi).

Trust is powerful. It is the glue that binds people together as they work in ambiguous, uncertain environments in ambiguous, uncertain times. It is also at the root of a leader's credibility or lack thereof. Without trust, 'honest communication' becomes a self-canceling oxymoron, while the stated goals of empowering people and pushing authority downward fall far short of their potential. Show me an organization marked by a lot of internal distrust, and I'll show you an organization in decline (Hararia 28-29). Jenny McCune in Management Review cites a survey of 17 million employees in 40 countries about what people value the work place (12). The survey yielded eight behaviors valued by people. Trust from management is high on the list.

- Treat others with uncompromising truth.
- Lavish trust on your associates.
- Mentor unselfishly.
- Be receptive to new ideas, regardless of their origin.
- Take personal risks for the organization's sake.
- Give credit where it is due.
- Do not touch dishonest dollars.
- Put the interest of others before your own (12).

William Miller and Stephen Rollnick place responsibility for tapping into employee talents and abilities, and thus their productivity, squarely on the shoulders of the leaders (top management). An organization cannot play the new game of intellectual capital unless senior managers step up to the challenge of growing intellectual capital. They must embrace the need to expand their own intelligence, promote their own innovativeness, and exercise high integrity to get the process going. Then, they can begin to inspire courage in others to embrace the uncertainty of change, make internal transitions and value the requirements of the new game. These aspects of fear, trust and integrity correspond closely with Herzberg's hygiene factors: supervision, working conditions, relationship with supervisors, ... company policies and administration. In fact, throughout the contemporary literature about workplace productivity there are recurring links to the motivation theories of Maslow and Herzberg. The names of the factors may change, and the lists may be put in different orders, but the basic principles of workplace motivation remain constant.

Gain the tools to become a wise master builder.

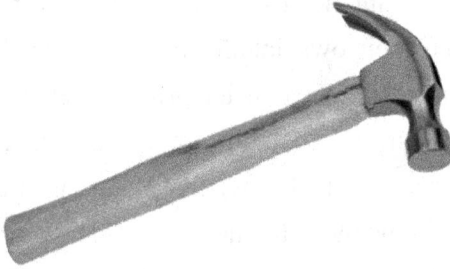

Chapter Three
Analysis Data

In 2004, Dr. Taylor Hartman's personality profile test was given to the staff members of Majesty International Center and Yahweh International. Below are the results gathered from twenty (20) staff members:

Results of Taylor Hartman's Color Code Test
Majesty International Center

Red	Blue	Yellow	White
4	3	6	7

Results of Taylor Hartman's Color Code Test
Yahweh International

Red	Blue	Yellow	White
5	8	2	5

The 20 staff members from each organization worked in different departments in the ministry. These findings were able to assist the management with the staff members' personalities and what type of character each staff member had. The essence of character is the ability to enhance not only our own lives, but the lives of others as well. Here, Dr. Hartman gives one the tools you need to unlock your true potential, including engaging case histories, clearly articulated principles, and step-by-step exercises for:

- Recognizing your innate -- and developed -- strengths
- Identifying your core motivations
- Communicating more effectively
- Focusing your commitments
- Discovering the importance of character "stretching"

Presented with refreshing style and candid professionalism, this revolutionary guide provides tremendous counsel for identifying and embracing an enhanced life.

The Color Code defines each color through core personality motives. Reds are driven by power, while Blues are motivated by intimacy. Whites seek peace, while Yellows clearly want to have fun. *Color Your Future* defines character as a learned process driven by the optimum motive of service. The more 'charactered' we become, the higher degree of trust we earn, and the greater amount of service we are able to render. Becoming 'charactered' requires a much more rigorous and principled process than merely having a personality, but offers a more powerful reward in the quality of one's life as well. It answers to a higher law than the basic motives of personality.

Unlike the unique personality motives, optimum character motives drive all personalities equally. For example, in order to serve others as dictated by our optimum motive, Yellow personalities, who innately prefer to play, must learn to focus their commitments. Reds are required to be less critical and more patient. Optimum motive demands acceptance and having realistic expectations of the Blues, while Whites are asked to confront their fears of interpersonal conflict and assert themselves. The optimum motive of service becomes our driving core in becoming 'charactered.'

In *The Color Code*, Taylor Hartman defined the characteristics of the four basic personality types and assigned a color to each. In this exciting sequel, he builds on his groundbreaking research, showing you how to use your color profile as a guide to cultivating a full and balanced character.

U.S. Army 23 Traits of Character

- Bearing
- Confidence
- Courage
- Integrity
- Decisiveness
- Justice
- Endurance
- Tact
- Initiative
- Coolness
- Maturity
- Improvement
- Will
- Assertiveness
- Candor
- Sense of humor
- Competence
- Commitment

- Creativity
- Self-discipline
- Humility
- Flexibility
- Empathy/Compassion

Leaders do not command excellence; they build excellence. Excellence is "being all you can be" within the bounds of doing what is right for your organization. To reach excellence, you must first be a leader of good character. You must do everything you are supposed to do. An organization will not achieve excellence by figuring out where it wants to go, then having leaders do whatever they have to in order to get the job done, and then hope their leaders acted with good character. This type of thinking is backwards.

Pursuing excellence should not be confused with accomplishing a job or task. When you plan, you do it by backwards planning. But you do not achieve excellence by backwards planning. Excellence starts with leaders of good and strong character who engage in the entire process of leadership. And the first process is being a person of honorable character.

"Waste no time arguing what a good man should be. Be one."
Marcus Aurelius

Character develops over time. Many think that much of a person's character is formed early in life. However, we do not know exactly how much or how early character develops. But, it is safe to claim that character does not change quickly. A person's observable behavior is an indication of his/her character. This behavior can be strong or weak, good or bad. A person with strong character shows drive, energy, determination, self-discipline, willpower, and nerve. He/she sees what he/she wants and goes after it. He/she attracts followers. On the other hand, a person with weak character shows none of these traits. He/she does not know what he/she wants. His/her traits are disorganized; she vacillates and is inconsistent. He/she will attract no followers.

A strong person can be good or bad. A gang leader is an example of a strong person with a bad character, while an outstanding community leader is one with both strong and good characteristics. An organization needs leaders with both strong and good characteristics, people who will guide them to the future and show that they can be trusted.

Courage- not complacency-is our need today.

"Leadership not salesmanship."
John F. Kennedy

To be an effective leader, your followers must have trust in you and they need to be sold on your vision. Korn-Ferry International, an executive search company, performed a survey on what organizations want from their leaders. The respondents said they wanted people who were both ethical and who convey a strong vision of the future. In any organization, a leader's actions set the pace. This behavior wins trust, loyalty, and ensures the organization's continued vitality. One of the ways to build trust is to display a good sense of character composed of beliefs, values, skills, and traits.

Beliefs are what we hold dear to us and are rooted deeply within us. They could be assumptions or convictions that you hold true regarding people, concepts, or things. They could be the beliefs about life, death, religion, what is good, what is bad, what is human nature, etc.

Values are attitudes about the worth of people, concepts, or things. For example, you might value a good car, home, friendship, personal comfort, or relatives. Values are important as they influence a person's behavior to weigh the importance of alternatives. For example, you might value friends more than privacy, while others might be the opposite.

Skills are the knowledge and abilities that a person gains throughout life. The ability to learn a new skill varies with each individual. Some skills come almost naturally, while others come only by complete devotion to study and practice.

Traits are distinguishing qualities or characteristics of a person, while character is the sum total of these traits. There are hundreds of personality traits, far too many to be discussed here. Instead, we will focus on a few that are crucial for a leader. The more of these you display as a leader, the more your followers will believe and trust in you.

Traits of a Good Leader
- Compiled by the Santa Clara University and the Tom Peters Group:

- Honesty- Display sincerity, integrity, and candor in all your actions. Deceptive behavior will not inspire trust.

- Competent- Your actions should be based on reason and moral principles. Do not make decisions based on childlike emotional desires or feelings.

- Forward-looking- Set goals and have a vision of the future. The vision must be owned throughout the organization. Effective leaders envision what they want and how to get it. They habitually pick priorities stemming from their basic values.

- Inspiring- Display confidence in all that you do. By showing endurance in mental, physical, and spiritual stamina, you will inspire others to reach for new heights. Take charge when necessary.

- Intelligent- Read, study, and seek challenging assignments.

- Fair-minded- Show fair treatment to all people. Prejudice is the enemy of justice. Display empathy by being sensitive to the feelings, values, interests, and wellbeing of others.

- Broad-minded- Seek out diversity.

- Courageous- Have the perseverance to accomplish a goal, regardless of the seemingly insurmountable obstacles. Display a confident calmness when under stress.

- Straightforward- Use sound judgment to make good decisions at the right time.

- Imaginative- Make timely and appropriate changes in your thinking, plans, and methods. Show creativity by thinking of new and better goals, ideas, and solutions to problems. Be innovative!

Attributes establish what leaders are, and every leader needs at least three of them:

Standard Bearers

establish the ethical framework within an organization. This demands a commitment to live and defend the climate and culture that you want to permeate your organization. What you set as an example will soon become the rule. Unlike knowledge, ethical behavior is learned more by observing than by listening. And in fast-moving situations, examples become certainty. Being a standard bearer creates trust and openness in your church members/employees, who in turn, fulfill your visions.

Developers

help others learn through teaching, training, and coaching. This creates an exciting place to work and learn. Never miss an opportunity to teach or learn something new yourself. Coaching suggests someone who cares enough to get involved by encouraging and developing others who are less experienced. Employees who work for developers know they can take risks, learn by making mistakes, and winning in the end.

Integrators

orchestrate the many activities that take place throughout an organization by providing a view of the future and the ability to obtain have a sixth sense about where problems will occur and make their presence felt during critical times. They know that their employees do their best when they are left to work within a vision-based framework.

Integrity

God wants leaders to be men of integrity.

"Now this is our boast: Our conscience testifies that we have conducted ourselves in the world, and especially in our relations with you, in the holiness and sincerity that are from God. We have done so not according to worldly wisdom but according to God's grace. For we do not write you anything you cannot read or understand."

2 Cor. 1:12-13

In this text, Paul declares he has no hidden agendas. He will not indulge in politicking nor does he plan to manipulate anyone. What you see is what you get. He means exactly what he says, nothing more. No need to examine the numerical value of the Greek letters to arrive at a hidden meaning.

The words used to translate 'holiness and sincerity' in the above verse show Paul means purity of motives and single-mindedness of purpose. Transparency of this sort is simply a question of integrity and takes time to develop.

Integrity is so closely related to humility that we might argue they are synonyms. It would take a better philosopher to make such distinctions. Let us agree they are indispensably linked.

Integrity is central to all leadership, religious or secular. Business analysts, such as Stephen Covey in his book, *Seven Habits of Effective People*, have recently 'discovered' the importance of character in business. This book has become a best seller.

Covey notes, however, a disturbing shift in attitudes toward character in leadership in western culture over the last 200 years. He classifies this shift as Character Ethic versus Personality Ethic. In the first 150 years of the history of the United States, philosophy of leadership emphasized the importance of traits like integrity, humility, fidelity, etc. Since World War II, the emphasis has been on personality traits as the key to success rather than ethics, *per se*. He notes:

Success became more a function of personality, of public image, of attitudes and behaviors, skills and techniques... Other parts of the personality approach were clearly manipulative, even deceptive, encouraging people to use techniques to get other people to like them...

Christians need to be aware of cultural shifts like this and carefully distinguish them from the traits Jesus calls for in those He chooses for leadership.

In his book *Good to Great*, researcher Jim Collins presents his analysis of companies, which grew from good to great and stayed there. He found a quality in common among the leaders of these companies, which had nothing to do with temperament: "We were surprised, shocked really, to discover the type of leadership required for turning a good company into a great one.... Self-effacing, quiet, reserved, even shy- these leaders are a paradoxical blend of personal humility and professional will."

Note the point: The key quality in common among leaders of companies who had moved from good to great was humility. He adds, "[These] leaders channel their ego needs away from themselves and into the larger goal of building a great company. It's not that [these] leaders have no ego or self-interest. Indeed, they are incredibly ambitious- but their ambition is first and foremost for the institution, not themselves."

Leadership of lasting value cannot exist without this virtue. Management, yes. Manipulation and control, yes...but not true leadership which buys the loyalty of others at the cost of pain to oneself. It is the integrity of Jesus. This is the Christian philosophy of leadership.

The Caiaphas Principle

Caiaphas was a man who sold his integrity for the price of peace. He was the high priest who presided over the trial of Jesus. In John 11:49b-50 we read: *"You know nothing at all! You do not realize that it is better for you that one man die for the people than that the whole nation perish."*

From Caiaphas' perspective, it was better to abandon his integrity by condemning an innocent man than risk widespread destruction by attracting the attention of their Roman overlords. Was he right? Yes, in the short run. He successfully averted Roman intervention and national disaster. He must have considered himself profoundly wise.

The long run, however, was different. Eventually, the Romans came and destroyed the nation anyway. He won in the short run but lost everything in the end, including his own honor. Jesus, on the other hand, seemed to lose in the short run. He was humiliated, crucified and seemed to disappear. Who is King of Kings today and where is Caiaphas?

Suppose you have a man in church caught in deep sin. You know you must discipline him. He is a very popular person, however, with wealth and influence. If you discipline him, it may divide the church. You might lose your job as pastor. What do you do?

This is a classic test of integrity. If you stand your ground, you may lose in the short run. The church might indeed be divided. You could lose your job. But, God will give you far more than you ever lost, and you will have no regrets. Integrity, which includes humility, is the foundation virtue of leadership. Without it, a 'leader' is no more than a manager at best and a manipulator and controller at worst. Even the worldly notice this.

The Three Key Attitudes

In the scenario described in Matthew Chapter 20, the mother of James and John approached Jesus asking that her sons sit beside Jesus in His Kingdom. This episode provided the opportunity for Jesus to introduce three key attitudes in Christian leadership: suffering, parity and service.

Suffering: The pressures of leadership are enormous. A leader must be prepared to suffer, often in secret, to fulfill his/her calling.

Parity: Ministers are equal in authority in the body of Christ. They relate to one another like knights at a round table rather than ranks in an army. Biblical government is an association of ministers, working together in mutual respect as equals. Complex authoritarian hierarchies have no place in God's Kingdom, are worldly in their conception, and lead to the very things for which Jesus rebuked these two disciples. (We'll see more about heirarchialism below.)

Service: Leaders have a servant attitude rather than a ruler attitude. People are the whole point of their work, not tools toward their own purposes.

What were James and John seeking and how did they go about it? They sought status and honor through manipulation. They assumed the Kingdom of God would be set up just like any other government, with Jesus as supreme ruler, followed by a series of ranks. Notice they mentioned nothing of actual work to accomplish, just ranks.

We can imagine them plotting, "You know, Jesus can be a little tough on us sometimes. He's really gentle with women, though. Let's see if we can get Mama to talk to Him and maybe work out a good deal for ourselves."

This is politicking and manipulation, standard procedure in the world's leadership paradigm. Notice Jesus does not rebuke them for ambition, because ambition is a good thing if it is for God's glory. He admonishes against seeking their own honor. Jesus also makes it clear He is not in charge of promotions in the personnel department. The Father is (v. 23). They were asking the wrong person. From this, we see a hint of the first principle of Christian leadership in the New Testament: It is a **gift** from God.

Nevertheless, these sons of Zebedee had two good qualities, although seriously misdirected:

Ambition: This is a good characteristic for a Christian if the ambition is directed toward the glory of God rather than our own sense of self-worth.

Confidence: Unfortunately, it was confidence in themselves rather than in God. "We are able." They considered themselves eminently "able." The garden of Gethsemane taught them otherwise. They abandoned Jesus and fled.

This brings up the first key attitude Jesus taught them.

FIRST KEY ATTITUDE: Suffering

"But Jesus answered and said, 'You do not know what you ask. Are you able to drink the cup that I am about to drink, and be baptized with the baptism that I am baptized with?' They said to Him, 'We are able'."

Matthew 20:22

The call to Christian leadership is a call to suffering. The 'suffering' involved, especially in the western world, usually takes the form of psychological pressures and stresses other believers neither bear nor understand.

Frequently, people have high expectations of a leader. They may be looking to a pastor to meet their needs rather than to Christ. When the pastor fails to meet their personal expectations, they may consider him/her incompetent. Some under his/her care may not be submissive and will only submit when pressured into it. Sometimes, the leader must hold the line on godly principles, risking the misunderstanding and criticism of others.

Occasionally, church leaders must apply biblical discipline when it may be unpopular to do so. When dealing with a disciplinary case, the leaders often cannot reveal the problem to the congregation. Members with incomplete knowledge of the case may draw wrong conclusions about the leaders' decisions. They may imagine the leaders are too harsh or too lax in discipline. The leaders may find themselves suffering in silence. God has wisely arranged it so.

Titles and honors that accompany the office of leader are insufficient to compensate for the stress. Those who highly value titles or honors more than the service entailed, soon find themselves disappointed and disillusioned.

Similarly, in his book, *Brothers, We Are Not Professionals*, John Piper attacks attitude of "professionalism in pastoral ministry which puts aside the embracing of suffering as requisite:

We pastors are being killed by the professionalizing of the pastoral ministry. The mentality of the professional is not...the mentality of the slave of Christ. Professionalism has nothing to do with the essence and heart of the Christian ministry... For there is no professional childlikeness (MT 18:3); there is no professional tenderheartedness (Eph.4:32); there is no professional panting after God (Ps.42:1)."

SECOND KEY ATTITUDE: Parity

"Jesus called them together and said, 'You know that the rulers of the Gentiles lord it over them, and their high officials exercise authority over them. Not so with you. Instead, whoever wants to become great among you must be your servant'."
Matthew 20:25

If you treat a person as an equal, assuming he/she is wise, he/she will defer to you in areas he/she knows you are knowledgeable.

Authoritarianism and hierarchialism support each other, and it is hard to tell which is the driving force. Do authoritarian people create hierarchies? Do dictatorial attitudes produce authoritarian attitudes? Regardless, authoritarianism is a by-product of arrogance. Authoritarian people often suppose their superior office proves they are inherently superior individuals. This is why they 'lord it over' others. They assume they have a natural right to do so.

Complex hierarchies are inevitable in the world. Armies are hierarchies, with their generals at the top, followed by colonels, majors, captains, and sergeants, down to privates. Likewise with corporations, the CEO is at the top, followed by vice presidents, department managers, all the way down to stock boys in the basement.

Hierarchies are necessary in such domains. Jesus is not teaching authoritarian hierarchies are wrong. He is simply saying, "Not so with you." The phrase, "Not so with you:" is literally in Greek, "It shall not be so among you." Jesus was speaking in Aramaic, a dialect of Hebrew. In that language, future tenses are used as imperatives. Jesus was probably saying, "I forbid you to put into office people with authoritarian attitudes and temperaments."

This excludes some "natural" leaders from Christian offices. Christian organizations often ignore this principle. Along comes a man/woman with natural leadership traits. Sure, he/she is a bit arrogant. He/she likes to control. Maybe, he/she is a bit overbearing at times, but so what? He/she has 'leadership' abilities. So, he/she gets authority in the organization. Result: Wounded people. Good people are lost and refuse to be the brunt of his/her arrogance.

Just because a man/woman has leadership ability does not mean he/she should be a leader in a Christian organization. If he/she tends toward authoritarian and controlling attitudes, he/she is the last person to be qualified. In their ranks, he/she must never be allowed to rise above the last one. Controllers must be controlled.

This may be what Jesus meant when He said, *"Whoever wants to become great among you must be your servant"* (Mark 10:43). Some scholars have interpreted this phrase to mean, 'Servant leadership is the way to get promoted in the Kingdom of God.' This interpretation may be valid. Considering the context however, it seems more likely a prohibition against appointing people with authoritarian attitudes. The point: Neither natural leadership ability nor experience in business or the military, nor profiles on a psychological test, are final indications a man/woman should be a candidate for Christian leadership. If he/she holds autocratic attitudes, thinks hierarchically or tends to use or abuse people, he/she is disqualified as a candidate, regardless of other considerations.

THIRD KEY ATTITUDE: Service

> *"...just as the Son of Man did not come to be served, but to serve and to give his life a ransom for many."*
>
> Mt. 20:28

Christian leadership focuses more on helping others than commanding them. It is a life given over to service. Many are attracted to Christian offices for the honors but wind up as negligent leaders, more concerned for their status than the welfare of the people. These do harm to themselves as well. Eccl. 8:9 says, *"There is a time in which one man rules over another to his own hurt."*

The goal of a Christian leader is to make his/her followers the best they can be. In fact, if he/she can train someone to replace him/her, this is the best leadership of all. Servant leadership is essential in the Kingdom of God because of the end product. In the business world, people are a resource to produce material goods. People give time and energy to produce something for public consumption, such as automobiles, pencils or whatever.

God's Kingdom uses material resources to produce sanctified people. The world considers this a non-issue. After all, sanctification is difficult to define, something only God can measure. Sanctified people are what the ministry is all about. Christian leadership involves a set of attitudes different from worldly systems. Embracing the inevitable suffering, whether psychological or physical, helps a leader put his/her own motives into perspective. Serving others to help them reach their full potential and treating fellow ministers as equals is more than the mere duties of an office. It is a way of life.

Good Christian leaders, functioning within a hierarchical system, try to mitigate these negative effects. These efforts are laudable, though often futile. Human nature, including among Christians, is susceptible to the temptations generated by hierarchical systems.

Hierarchies Tend to Stimulate the Worst in Fallen Human Nature

This includes Christian hierarchies. Some of these aspects are:

A. Arrogance

People tend to want to feel superior to others. Hierarchies provide for this by giving ranks, one superior to the other. The assumption is, "I have a superior rank because I am a superior person."

B. Unholy Ambition and Jealousy

A person sees another in a rank above his/her and says to him/herself, "He is no better than I. In fact, I can do his job better. So, why shouldn't I have that rank?"

C. Dirty Politicking

If a person wants a superior rank, he/she may be tempted to try to pull strings and make deals to get it. This is morally questionable and a wasteful effort that could be spent in productive work. The Apostle James notes, *"For where you have envy and selfish ambition, there you find disorder and every evil practice"* (James 3:16). The term evil practice translates phaulon pragma, literally 'foul business.' The modern phrase, 'dirty politicking' expresses it well.

D. Blame Shifting

This is a form of moral cowardice. Human nature has a tendency to blame a subordinate when something goes wrong. Blame shifting was Adam's first reaction after the fall (Genesis Chapter 3). Imagine a man carrying a load up a ladder. If the man on the top drops his load, where does it go? On the man beneath, who dumps it on the man below him? The guy on the bottom gets the full load. In a hierarchy, the load is the blame.

E. Man-Pleasing

Since a person's rank in the hierarchy depends on the good will of the rank above him, this tempts him to focus on pleasing the man above rather than pleasing God.

F. Loss of Competent Personnel

According to Dr. Peter, in *The Peter Principle*, hierarchies tend to squeeze out people who question the way things are done, even if they are highly competent. A hierarchy, like any organism, becomes more focused on perpetuating its own existence than to what it was created to produce. People who 'rock the boat' will be thrown out of that boat. It does not matter if they were among the few doing the rowing.

G. Disregard of the Spiritual Authority of Ordained Offices

In a Christian hierarchy, leaders sometimes act as though their man-made title or ranks negates the spiritual authority of biblical ones. The Word of God affords certain rights and privileges to all ordained officers in the body of Christ. Hierarchical structures overlook these. According to Scripture, God's ordained leaders have certain rights and privileges, which no one may disregard without due process.

Our current culture tends toward independence, individualism, and a distrust of institutions. These attitudes may cause a disregard of the spiritual authority God gives ministers. If church members submit to them, they may do so because they like them, not because they respect the office or acknowledge their spiritual authority.

Worse, we as ordained ministers might inadvertently violate the rights of our fellow ministers. We may end up treating our colleagues as less than what the Word of God says they are. If we understand the rights of ministers, we can avoid treating our fellow ministers unethically. One of these rights and privileges is:

The Right to Respect
"Let the elders who rule well be counted worthy of double honor, especially those who labor in the word and doctrine."
1 Tim. 5:17

The preaching and teaching of the Word is so central to Christian ministry, we must be careful to honor those called to it. This includes avoiding derogatory comments about a fellow minister. There are exceptions, nevertheless. We have the right and mandate to speak against heretics, whether they *call* themselves ministers or not. In fact, these are not fellow ministers (Rom. 16: 17-18).

Disciplinary cases involving ministers is another exception. So is evaluating a fellow minister for consideration for future work. Negative evaluations may be correct in such a setting. We treat fellow ministers as equals, because that is what they are before God. (In Reformed Ecclesiology, there is no other rank higher than the ordained minister in this dispensation. Some ministers have earned more respect than others because of their experience or accomplishments. But under no circumstances are we to treat any minister as less than a minister of Christ.)

Conversely, this means ministers have a right to defend themselves against abuses from others, when necessary to do so for the honor of the gospel. This is the entire point behind II Corinthians as well as I Corinthians Chapter 4. Paul had to defend against a disdainful attitude from the Corinthian believers. He did this not for his sake alone, but for the honor of the gospel and because their attitude was sinful.

Being a servant predisposed to suffering does not always mean a leader must let him/herself be walked on. When the honor of the gospel is called into question, he/she not only has a right to defend him/herself, he/she has that obligation.

Functional Aspects of Leadership

a) The Great Myth of Christian Leadership:

When God wants a leader, He looks down over a group of His children and chooses the one with a special gift of wisdom, along with profound spirituality. This is why God chooses some and not others.

The above paragraph is a myth. The term 'elder' in Scripture derived its meaning from the maturity normally associated with years of experience. Regardless of a man's age, we expect him to possess the wisdom, maturity and humility of an 'elder.'

The point: promotion to leadership is a gift of God's grace. No one ever fully deserves it.

The Apostle Paul says in I Cor. 15:10, *"But by the grace of God I am what I am, and his grace to me was not without effect. No, I worked harder than all of them yet not I, but the grace of God that was with me."*

Did Paul, therefore, deserve to be an apostle? No. It was the grace of God alone who called and qualified him. There is no function in the Kingdom of God we are big enough for without His grace. [19]

b) The Gift of Leadership

The Bible indicates Christian leadership is a gift of the Spirit.
"We have different gifts, according to the grace given us... (8)... if it is leadership, let him govern diligently; ..."
Rom. 12:6

Although the spiritual gift of leadership may accompany a natural gift, God is not dependent on natural human talents. He calls some to it despite reluctance on their part. Moses was an example of this. His first reaction was to make excuses for rejecting the call (Ex. 3:11-12).

c) The Phenomenon of Spiritual Authority

Defining spiritual authority is like pinning down the meaning of "anointing." We may not know what it is, but we sure know what it isn't! Spiritual authority is the testimony of God about the authenticity of a leader, along with the conviction that one ought to esteem to his/her ministry. This is what was taking place when the Father spoke to the disciples about Jesus, *"This is my Son, whom I have chosen; listen to him"* (Luke 9:35).

d) The Leader's Function

> *"Keep watch over yourselves and all the flock of which the Holy Spirit has made you overseers. Be shepherds of the church of God, which he bought with his own blood."*
>
> Acts 20:28

This verse is perhaps the richest description of the Christian leader's responsibility in the entire Bible. Note these particulars: The leader's first spiritual concern must be for him/herself. This sounds surprising but it is true. "Keep watch over yourselves" means the leader is to attend to his/her own spiritual welfare first. He/she must carefully maintain a solid and consistent devotional life. A chief trap of Satan is to get us so busy we neglect prayer and fellowship with God through the Word. Many a leader has fallen because he/she has gotten so busy in the ministry, he/she has neglected his/her own soul and left him/herself an easy target for the enemy.

The calling is from God. Though we qualify to be ordained in Christian organizations, in the final analysis, it is the Spirit who makes us *"overseers."* *"Be shepherds"* translates the Greek verb POIMAINO. This verb means *"to lead, with the implication of providing for, 'to guide and to help, to guide and take care of.'* It also means, *"to rule, with the implication of direct personal involvement"* [21].

Notice the term definitely includes authority. A Christian leader is not there merely to make suggestions. He/she has authority from God to be directly involved in the personal lives of the sheep. He/she feeds the sheep by providing them the Word of God. *"Bought with his own blood."* Paul adds this to emphasize the supreme value and importance of spiritual leadership. No occupation or function in the world could possibly be more important because nothing else could cost a higher price than the blood of Christ.

In short, the leader's function is to shepherd. People are more important than programs, plans or procedures. In our present technological society, we may easily lose sight of this central fact.

e) The Leader's Strategy

"It was he who gave some to be apostles, some to be prophets, some to be evangelists, and some to be pastors and teachers, to prepare God's people for works of service, so that the body of Christ may be built up."

Eph. 4:11-12

Training the church to do the work of the ministry is the leader's strategy. Who does the work of the ministry according to the text above? God's people. The church members.

Everyone in the church should have a job. The leader's role is to be a supervisor. That's what 'bishop' means. He is 'overseer' or 'supervisor.' (Gk. 'Episkopos' Epi means 'upon' and skopos means 'look.' It refers to one who watches over the activities of another.)

Suppose one were looking for a construction crew to build a house for him. He/she goes to a construction site where he/she had heard a crew is working. There, notice a group of workers standing around in a circle, shovels in hand, with a supervisor in the middle. The supervisor is digging laboriously. All the workers are applauding and saying, "Go, boss! Keep up the good work. You're doing a fine job!"

What would one think of a crew like that? Would they be considered to build the house? Unfortunately, many churches function this way. The church sits and applauds while the pastor does all the preaching, teaching, visitation, counseling and correcting. They praise his/her efforts, and it never enters their heads they should be doing any of those things. Pastors end up suffering a high percentage of heart attacks.

A classic trap for the fledgling leader is to focus on the weakest members rather than the strongest. After all, they seem the most needy. The discerning leader spends his/her time preparing the strong to help the weak. The big danger for the novice leader is assuming his/her job is to heal all the wounded, sooth all the hurt feelings, and support the weak. (This is like trying to feed all the poor, which Jesus said is impossible. It never ends.)

Such a trap duplicates a fundamental teaching error sometimes committed in the public schools, lowering your standards to accommodate the weakest student. The result is poor education. If a leader has the wisdom to invest in potential people, rather than problem people, he/she will discover he/she is training those who can minister to the problem people.

f) The Leader's Principal Product

"And the things you have heard me say in the presence of many witnesses entrust to reliable men who will also be qualified to teach others."

2 Ti. 2:2

The main thing a Christian leader should produce is other leaders. That is how Paul's friend Timothy ended up in the ministry. Some pastors seem reluctant to prepare other people in their congregation for leadership. Having known many pastors, I may suspect some fear others may rise to take their place and they would be out of a job. Rather than take the risk, they prefer the congregation as a whole remain mediocre.

Evangelist Leighton Ford notes how some strong leaders fail to develop the leadership under them, with long-term disastrous results: Perhaps some of the first-generation leaders saw the second-generation leaders as unwelcome competitors and did not set out to develop them. An Indian proverb says, "Nothing grows under a Banyan tree." Often the shadow of these strong leaders was so large that the little seedlings were not nurtured under them." Observation and experience shows God always promotes to greater ministry leaders who prepare others to take their place.

Planning Within the Local Church Setting

In the local church, the leaders need to establish vision and goals. A church without a vision statement and clear goals will likely go nowhere. Annual planning is a must for a church. Example: Suppose young families are moving into a community. One's goal is to reach for Christ five of these new families during the next year. A church board has embraced this challenge and announced this goal to the congregation. What now?

A. Review the goal with your people regularly, asking for their creative input. This helps them 'own' the goal. Set fixed dates to review your 'goal progress'. If you have a goal for this year, for example, then set dates every two months to review results. This helps keep everyone on track.

B. Be prepared for opposition. There will always be dissenters, no matter what. Example: One's goal is to win five young couples to the Lord. Then, one Sunday someone approaches them in the church and says, "A group of us would like to start a ministry to the elderly in the nursing home." How should you respond?

You might say, "That's a laudable goal, but how does it fit in with our vision this year of incorporating five young couples into the church? Show me how your idea fits in with the vision of the church; then, we can approve it. Otherwise, no." Doing this helps your members stay focused on the task without getting sidetracked. Problems inevitably spring up in the church, which tends to absorb one's time. Watch out for this.

Creative Thinking

One can define creative thinking as the ability to invent original ideas for accomplishing goals. The source of creative thinking is our imagination. This is a faculty of mind given by God, which He expects us to use. Guidance from God often comes through the application of our own mental faculties.

Why Are We Not Better at Creative Thinking?

A. Laziness.

Thinking is hard work. Creative thinking is hardest of all. Just ask a novelist. Most will tell you they only write three or four hours a day because it is too exhausting.

B. Wrong Theology About Guidance.

Christians sometimes have wrong concepts about the mind. They wait for God to give divine revelation, while God waits for them to use the faculties He gave them. Result: Nobody is moving, and nothing gets accomplished.

C. Repression of Creative Faculties.

A high-school teacher put a small dot on the blackboard. Then, he asked the class what it was. The students all agreed that is was nothing but a dot of chalk on the blackboard. The teacher replied, "I did the same exercise yesterday with a group of children. One thought it was an insect egg or perhaps a bird's eye. Another thought it was the head of a bald man seen from an airplane."

Why the difference? In the years between kindergarten and high school students were discarding their imagination. Why? Because they were learning to be 'specific' about things, learning the 'right answers' and learning what is 'realistic.'

Absorbing facts is not the same as exercising the mind. In some countries, the education system is based on rote memorization. Students write down verbatim what the teacher says, then copy it neatly into a notebook at home. This is supposed to be 'education.' It is not education. It is brainwashing.

D. Fear of Failure or Ridicule.

Nobody wants to make a fool of him/herself. The temptation toward this becomes stronger as we advance in leader-ship. We think, "If my new idea fails, we'll look like fools and people will lose confidence in us.

E. Negative Thinking.

What is the difference between a leader who gets things done and those who only manage the work of others? The former ignores the reasons why it can't be done and does it anyway.

Great entrepreneurs rarely ask, "Is this going to work?" Instead, they are challenged by, "How can we make it work?"

F. Comfort Zone

We confine ourselves to comfortable limitations. It seems so much easier to do the familiar. Sometimes, it is good to stretch out of our 'comfort zone' and attempt what we may not feel 'gifted' in.

Group Brainstorming

At a meeting in a paint company, technicians were seeking new ideas for removing paint. One man humorously suggested mixing dynamite with the paint. That way, years later, they could toss a match at the painted wall and blow it off. Once the laughter died down, the group took this bizarre idea and came up with a surprising solution: Mix a chemical with the paint, which could react later with the paint if pasted over it to dissolve it. This is how paint remover was invented. Is there any reason a group of Christians cannot excel in brainstorming? A stroke of genius is sometimes modified stupidity. Knowing this may help us break through inhibitions.

Tips for Good Relationships Among Ministers

A. The Mutual Defense Pact Among Leaders

Two or more leaders can make an agreement among themselves to defend each other when one is verbally attacked, especially in his/her absence. This presents a united front, which tends to silence critics. They learn that if they want to verbally attack your colleagues, they had better do it outside of your hearing.

What if the critic is correct in his/her assertion? Tell him/her the other ministers or leaders are capable of dealing with the matter. God frequently defends the leader even when the man is wrong in a decision. It seems God defends His own honor in such cases because He is the one who appointed the man. Leaders must beware of pride at this point. Some leaders assume a positive outcome is God's stamp of approval on their decisions. This can be self-deception.

B. Integrity, Not Control

I do not control other people nor allow others to control me. Is this attitude arrogant and independent? Not if integrity is the foundation of your relationships with those in authority over you. "Control" is one way leaders might relate to people, but it is not a godly one. The godly way is on another basis: integrity.

C. Keeping Agreements

When we give our word, we keep it even if it is inconvenient. The psalmist says the man is blessed *"who keeps his oath even when it hurts"* (Ps. 15:4). We keep our promises because we are made in the image of God, and He keeps His Word. Nothing is wrong with asking someone to renegotiate an agreement because of unforeseen factors. We do not, however, have the moral right to break it just because we may have the power or 'authority' to do so.

This is doubly true in relationships with ministerial colleagues. If you become a Christian leader in a powerful organization, the temptation may be to break inconvenient agreements simply because you have the power to get away with it. The power to do a thing and the right to do it are different issues. Beware of this human tendency if you become a leader in an influential organization. If you make agreements, do your best to keep them. Otherwise, it will erode your integrity, which ultimately means eroding your right to lead.

D. Accountability Groups

Every leader needs to be accountable to somebody, whether the system he/she is in requires it or not. Pick out two, or at the most, three friends who will agree to be an accountability group for you. This means you will keep them advised of important issues affecting you and will listen to their counsel. Prov. 24:6 says, *"and in a multitude of counsellors there is safety"* (KJV).

Chapter Four
Servant Leadership

This section presents the data in an objective manner. The purpose of this qualitative, descriptive research study was intended to observe the new phenomenon of the executive pastor by identifying the self-perceived leadership and management competencies important for local church administration. Additional information was collected to provide insight into the degree of job satisfaction, performance, and preparation for the any given position within a church for any department. The points below can be used by any department to identify what type of management skills the leader has or to evaluate any worker to see how productive he/she is.

1. Establishing work standards for your subordinates. (Directing & Controlling)
2. Training subordinates. (Training)
3. Management of your time at work. (Availability)
4. Communication of organizational goals and objectives to others. (Communication)
5. Organizing the workplace. (Organizing)
6. Helping subordinates to become and stay motivated. (Leading)
7. Availability to meet with your subordinates. (Availability)

8. Delegation of work to your subordinates. (Leading & Directing)
9. Quality of communication between you and your subordinates. (Communication)
10. How well you recognize your subordinates' performance. (Leading & Controlling)
11. Planning your section's work. (Planning)
12. Setting priorities for others who work for you. (Organizing, Leading & Directing)
13. Measuring work performance of your subordinates. (Controlling)
14. Your enjoyment of your job.
15. Your level of satisfaction with your own job performance.
16. Overall quality of the work you perform.
17. Openness of communication with management. (Reflects level of communication.)
18. Level of teamwork. (An indicator of leadership ability.)
19. Overall motivation towards their work. (Respect for the work force.)
20. Willingness to change. (Worker acceptance of the supervisor.)
21. Acceptance of responsibility. (A measure of supervisory trust.)
22. Management of their time. (Respect for the work force.)
23. Innovation and creativity. (Respect for the work force.)
24. Support of the unit or section's goals. (Respect for the work force.)
25. Maintenance of high standards. (Respect for the work force.)

26. Trust of management. (Respect for the work force.)
27. General attitude toward their work. (Respect for the work force.)
28. Spirit of cooperation with each other. (Respect for the work force.)
29. Ability to work without close supervision. (A measure of supervisory trust.)
30. Overall quality of their work. (Respect for the work force.)
31. Overall work force productivity. (Respect for the work force.)

The scaled items in this part were selected to reflect the effects of managerial actions (planning, organizing, directing, communicating, controlling, leading, training, recognizing, and the availability of management) as possibly perceived by persons in supervisory positions. My personal experience as a supervisor for the past thirty years influenced the selection of the items and their wording. The items reflect areas of subordinate performance frequently criticized by supervisors. The intent of including them here was to provide the respondents with thought provoking examples of potential problems and to give the supervisors the opportunity to praise or blame their subordinates.

Because the work force had indicated management as the cause of limited productivity, this set of items would enable the supervisors to reciprocate, thus, reinforcing the perception that communication and trust issues were dominant; or, the supervisors might not mirror the disdain of the work force, thus, leaving open alternative conclusions about the groups' perceptions of mutual communications and trust. Items 17-25 are related to actual work force job performance issues. The ratings for these items reflect the supervisor's respect of the work force. Items 25-28 reflect supervisory perceptions of workers' attitudes toward their jobs: also, an indicator of respect. Item 29 addresses whether the supervisors trust their subordinates, and items 30 and 31 give the supervisors the opportunity to laude or criticize their subordinates' overall performance. Part of the rationale for including these last two items is the philosophy espoused by Fournies: "Your ability as a manager is measured by what your subordinates do, not by what you do. Therefore, the facts of life dictate that, as a manager, you don't get paid for what you do, you get paid for what your subordinates do" (9). By extension, this philosophy dictates that any management behavior that does not support the workforce is self-destructive.

A leader can also use the points below to evaluate the workers or team players to see what Directive, Policy, Operating Procedure, or Situation Most Limits the Ability to Perform the Most Productive Work. This question asks the respondents to identify what limits their ability to do a good job. The factors identified indicate what the member feels limits his/her productivity. Although the factors vary between the surveys, there is also considerable agreement concerning the primary factors identified. This might refer to inadequate management and uncertain priorities or policies.

- Poor Management
- Poor, unavailable management
- Uncertain Priorities
- Politics

- Poor Communications
- Workload
- Lack of Recognition
- Computer problems
- Lack of Training
- Interruptions, meetings
- Poor Budgets
- Lack of knowledge/training
- Insufficient work force

Biblical Theology of Servant Leadership

As discussed in Chapter One, servant leadership is one of the foundations of building a strong team in the ministry. To build a biblical theology of servant leadership, one must define biblical theology, leadership, and servant leadership. An assessment of the biblical concepts and principles that define leadership is also required. These components exist within the text of this section. The result of the final analysis is a list of the important biblical principles uncovered during research. Significant New Testament personalities and events are examined and major concepts are discussed in order to build a framework for understanding biblical servant leadership.

John Maxwell provides the most basic definition of leadership: "Leadership is influence, nothing more, nothing less" (13). Daniel Katz and Robert Kahn provide a more industrial definition: "Leadership is the influential increment over and above mechanical compliance with the routine directives of the organization" (528).

These definitions of leadership give boundaries to leadership practices. Leadership is different from management or even administration. Leadership and management must coexist, as neither is truly possible without the other. Leadership focuses on doing the right things, while management focuses on doing things right. Administration can be defined as the processes and procedures that support the leadership and management process. The ultimate goal of those in authority is to do the right things right.

One way to look at this is that leadership without management will lead to frustration while management without leadership will lead to oppression. The competencies mentioned here are related to leadership, but they have application to management and administrative practices that assist in the organization's operation. The assumption that proper leadership models are appropriate for the church may be extended to management and administration, but that is not within the scope of this reference tool.

Servant leadership is another term that must be clear before proceeding with the foundational survey. There have been attempts to explain servant leadership. Just as there is much difficulty and confusion in delineating between management and leadership, understanding the relationship of servant leadership to leadership in general is also a problem. Some see servant leadership as a style of leadership. Servant leadership is best defined as a worldview or attitude of leading others from a perspective of placing the organizational purpose, the needs of the organization, and the needs of people over the needs and desires of the leader.

Robert Greenleaf, a veteran of many years of secular corporate management and leadership development, provides an excellent starting place for understanding a servant leadership definition. He states:

> The servant-leader is servant first... It begins with the natural feeling   that one wants to serve, to serve first. Then conscious choice brings one to aspire to lead. That person is sharply different from the one who is leader first, perhaps because of the need to assuage an unusual power drive or to acquire material possessions. For such it will be a later choice to serve- after leadership is established. The leader-first and the servant-first are two extreme types. Between them there are shadings and blends that are part of the infinite variety of human nature.
>
> The difference manifests itself in the care taken by the servant-first to make sure that other people's highest priority needs are being served. The best test, and most difficult to administer, is: Do those served grow as persons? Do they, while being served, become healthier, wiser, freer, more autonomous, more likely themselves to become servants? And, what is the effect on the least privileged in society; will they benefit, or, at least, will they not be further deprived? (Greenleaf 13).

Larry Spears, the CEO of the Greenleaf Center, who has extensive background in higher education, makes these additionally clarifying remarks concerning servant leadership.

As we near the end of the twentieth century, we are beginning to see that traditional autocratic and hierarchical modes of leadership are slowly yielding to a newer model -one that attempts to simultaneously enhance the personal growth of workers and improve the quality and caring of our many institutions through a combination of teamwork and community, personal involvement in decision making, and ethical and caring behavior. This emerging approach to leadership and service is called servant leadership (Spears & De Pree ii).

Lawrence Richards, who has experience in religious higher education and non-profit ministries, and Clyde Hoeldtke, an entrepreneur of a large privately-held business and one who is actively involved in local church ministries, provide a definition of servant leadership in this way.

The New Testament's picture of the servant as one who does rather than one who adopts the leadership style of the world has a unique integrity. The Christian both hears the Word from his/her spiritual leader and sees the Word expressed in his/her person. The open life of leaders among- not over - the brothers and sisters is a revelation of the very face of Jesus. And to see Jesus expressing Himself in a human being brings the hope that transformation might be possible for us too (Richards & Hoeldtke 120).

Henri J. M. Nouwen, a prolific writer on matters of spirituality and leadership, seeks a new type of leader for today and contrasts secular and servant leadership models in this statement.

The world in which we live - a world of efficiency and control - has no models to offer those who want to be shepherds in the way Jesus was a shepherd.... a whole new type of leadership is asked for in the church of tomorrow, a leadership which is not modeled on the power games of the world, but on the servant-leader, Jesus, who came to give His life for the salvation of many (Nouwen 44-45).

These are examples of ways to define leadership in a Christian or spiritual context. As a biblical theology of servant leadership is sought, these definitions will be used to guide the search for the overarching principles of servant leadership as presented in Scripture. What does the New Testament say about leadership? Is one style of leadership promoted over another? This section posits that the overarching theme of leadership espoused in the New Testament is based on servant hood. Within the context of the New Testament, a deductive process is used to determine what Scripture says specifically about servant leadership. The gospels provide pre-resurrection examples of servant leadership that are considered. Additionally, the New Testament provides the first examples of how the church after the resurrection was structured and operated. Various personalities are considered as examples or models of New Testament servant leadership. The words and examples of Jesus Christ are a prime source of information.

The Example of Jesus

As a leader seeks or takes on the role of responsibility, the examples of Christ are the greatest models of thought and action. Jesus was a leader to His people and is a leader for all mankind. He suffered for those He led; He placed others before

Himself and showed the world how a leader can be a serving minister.

As one analyzes the New Testament in search of servant leadership principles, the first example is Matthew 4:1-10. Jesus was in the midst of being tempted by the devil. After fasting for forty days and nights, Christ was hungry. The tempter came to Him and tempted Him with food first, protection second, and then with power and position. Christ's example here is to worship God and serve only Him. The lesson is that man is to put the worship of God over everything else. Matthew 6:1-5 provides an example for servant leaders to avoid acts that draw attention to themselves. This practice exudes from the individual the idea of the future reward from one's Father in Heaven. The concept here is the opposite of selling oneself and one's accomplishments. The idea is of being humble and private in one's accomplishments.

A servant leader should strive to serve others from a leadership position with anonymity. Allowing others to receive credit for their own work and providing opportunity for colleagues and workers to be successful can be learned from this passage.

In Matthew 10:24-25, one gets a picture of how a follower of Christ should consider himself. Jesus Christ was persecuted while on earth. Jesus was also the prime example of servant leadership. The concept here is that we are His disciples, and the disciple will not improve upon the Master's example. People in the first century cursed Christ. His followers should expect the same treatment. This is paralleled in Acts 5:41, where the disciples rejoiced that they were considered worthy to suffer beatings in their service to Christ.

Additionally, Philippians 3:10 supports this idea of sharing in the suffering of Christ as His servant. Servant leaders should anticipate the same treatment as Christ rather than seeking comfort and safety from an isolated leader position. Servant leaders will take on the less desirable work of leadership when they come alongside workers and followers. A practical application of this thought is that a leader should never ask a follower to do anything that the leader him/herself would not attempt.

Jesus left no one in doubt concerning the nature and character of the kingdom He came to establish. In John 18:26, He declared, *"My kingdom is not of this world."* Because His kingdom is not of this world, its leadership, both in principle and in practice was not to be patterned according to the worldly perception of leadership. Leadership in the perception of the world is a road to preeminence and "stardom," a survival of the fittest. But servant leadership, which Christ embodied, is a contrast to the world's understanding of leadership. It is the survival of the weakest (Akuchie 39).

We can see from the beginning what happens in an organization when someone presupposes their level of importance over the rest of the team. The rest of their colleagues became indignant with this request. Jesus was able to make this a teachable moment by showing how self-promotion is counter to a servant leadership style. First of all, in the situation with James and John, the mother and her two sons were seeking their own will rather than the will of God.

According to Matthew 20:22, they did not understand what they were asking. They were also attempting a takeover of the leadership reward. This is paralleled to how the world views leadership. One must get what he/she can before someone else takes the prize. James and John were exhibiting behavior that was selfish rather than selfless. Jesus used this situation to provide a contrast between secular leadership and servant leadership.

Jesus called them together and said in Matthew 20:25-28:

You know that the rulers of the Gentiles lord it over them, and their high officials exercise authority over them. Not so with you. Instead, whoever wants to become great among you must be your servant, and whoever wants to be first must be your slave- just as the Son of Man did not come to be served, but to serve, and to give His life as a ransom for many.

This passage not only clears up the difference between leadership styles, but it also makes a clear statement about what Jesus Christ's purpose is regarding servanthood. He came to serve, rather than be served. The lesson in this case is for leaders to be servants.

The Mystery of Christ's Leadership

Even the first followers of Christ were confused about the meaning of Christ's purpose. The first century Jews were looking for a leader to free them from the political bondage of Rome. In seeking this liberator, John the Baptist asked Jesus the question, *"Are you the one who was to come, or should we expect someone else?"* (Matt 11:2-6; Luke 7:19-23). Even John had been asked this question by the religious leaders of his day who were looking for the one who would lead them to freedom (John 1:19-27). At the last appearing of Christ, the disciples asked once more, *"Lord, are you at this time going to restore the kingdom of Israel?"* (Acts 1:6). Until the very last day, the disciples were looking for the one to free them from political rule. Jesus came for another reason.

Ndubuisi Akuchie states: Jesus came into the world as a leader at a time when His people needed leadership most. However, the character of His leadership was contradictory to the popular expectation. It was so enigmatic that He was rejected by His people as their messiah and the eschatological liberator of Deuteronomy 18:15 (39).

What was true with the New Testament writers is true today. It is difficult for mankind to understand and accept the concept of servanthood as a foundation for leadership. We default to absorbing secular leadership as the worldview rather than building upon servanthood as an identity with Christ.

These people were seeking a strong leader to vanquish the political and social oppression of Rome. In the minds of these Jews, Jesus was their answer. Today, many leaders aspire to this same level of position. Individuals want to be the strong and brave leader with the power, control, and prestige that accompany the position. There is nothing wrong with gaining the highest level of leadership or having strong skills and abilities that undergird successful leadership and management. What Christ is showing in this passage is that the primary goal of one who follows Him is to serve. If one seeks to attain a level of leadership and follow Christ's example, then servanthood is required. Servant leadership is discussed and exhibited frequently in both the Old and New Testaments. A clear statement is provided by Christ Himself in this encounter with the mother of James and John. As the supreme example, Jesus Christ said He came to serve rather than to be served (Matt. 20:20-28). His ultimate act as a servant leader was to love people so much that even though they were sinners and rejected Him, He still died for them.

Providing additional light on Matthew 20:20-28, Lawrence Richards and Clyde Hoeldtke state:

This passage attacks many of our ingrained assumptions about leadership and helps us define how a servant leads. Servant leadership is a practical philosophy, which supports people who choose to serve first, and then lead as a way of expanding service to individuals and institutions. Servant leaders may or may not hold formal leadership positions. Servant leadership encourages collaboration, trust, foresight, listening, and the ethical use of power and empowerment (106).

Summary of a Theology of Servant Leadership

After briefly reviewing many New Testament passages regarding servant leadership, what conclusions can be reached? There are guiding principles from every area of Scripture regarding how a leader, especially one who is a servant, should act. These are defined as overarching principles of servant leadership. Gangel provides a framework for this discussion through his analysis of servant leadership in the New Testament. The derived principles define leadership as servant-hood, stewardship, shared power, ministry, modeling behavior, and membership in the body of Christ (25-29). This framework is used to guide the analysis of this biblical theology of New Testament servant leadership.

Leadership is servanthood. The servant leader is to strive to lead through service, rather than climb for the highest level of leadership. A servant is someone who does not exert his/her own importance, but the importance of others. A true servant leader accepts responsibility as a means to greater service. Kouzes and Posner reinforce this idea from a secular standpoint through love and ensuring self-leadership. Kouzes and Posner illustrate love this way: " ... being in love with leading, with the people who do the work, with what their organizations produce, and with those who honor the organization by using its work" (305).

These concepts also promote a servant's heart similar to Greenleaf as they espouse five ways to share power and influence: "Strengthening others: ensuring self leadership, providing choice, developing competence, assigning critical tasks, and offering visible support" (185). A true servant helps others achieve their own level of competence in servant leadership. Assisting others to be employable rather than employed is a way secular for-profit and non-profit organi-zations can be servants to their workers.

Leadership is stewardship. Minister is defined as "a servant" in Matthew 20:26. One sees here that Christians are to be good stewards or managers of those things that God has entrusted to them. In the parable of the steward and in Paul's words in 1 Corinthians 4:2, one sees that Christians are being entrusted with certain responsibilities for which they are accountable to God. In general management, this can be defined as stewardship as well. Peter Block makes the following statement regarding choosing service over self-interest. "Stewardship is defined ... as the willingness to be accountable for the well-being of the larger organization by operating in service rather than in control, of those around us. Stated simply, it is accountability without control or compliance" (xx). He continues, "There is pride in leadership; it evokes images of direction. There is humility in stewardship; it evokes images of service. Service is central to the idea of stewardship" (Block 41). A servant leader is responsible to the Master's will. He/she operates with the understanding that the Master will return. The servant leader does every task as if he/she is serving the Master specifically and personally.

Leadership is shared power. One can see that this is an important principle in the definition of servant leadership, generally and specifically in the examples of Barnabas and Paul as they develop new leaders. Empowerment is the word used in secular circles. Peter Block states, "Empowerment is a state of mind as well as a result of position, policies, and practices. As managers, we become more powerful as we nurture the power of those below us. One way we nurture those below us is by becoming a role model for how we want them to function" (Block, 1987, 68). This definition of empowerment and how the leaders should respond in organizations show similarities with the biblical approach.

As leaders nurture those in churches or other church-based organizations, leaders spread information and learning. Leaders will also begin to develop new leaders sooner. If leaders model the way they want people to behave, then leaders will create their own accountability systems for maintaining the shared power idea. Empowerment may not fully define the biblical meaning of the concept of shared power. Empowerment in management terms means that some other person has given us power. This is true in organizations, but is different in the Christian life. Jesus Christ gives us our power, not another person. Servant leaders will do well to remember that every believer has been empowered by God.

Leadership is ministry. This is another of Gangel's derived principles. This has been discussed in light of stewardship. There are some additional comments that can be made. Christians are called to work together to serve. If people are serving each other diligently, without selfishness, then the acts of ministry will in turn strengthen the fabric of organizations. As Gangel puts it, "The smog of selfishness and egoism lifts to make mutual ministry a biblical reality" (29).

Richards and Hoeldtke provide additional counsel by stating: "Leaders in the body of Christ should never forsake the role of servants. Even when they are opposed to a plan or program, they are not permitted to demand, but must remain gentle in the instruction and rely on the head of the body to change the hearts of their opponents (or their own)" (102).

Leadership is modeling behavior. Examples of the disciples have been discussed, but the major example of leading by modeling is in the person of Christ. Richards and Hoeldtke define modeling succinctly: "The spiritual leader who is a servant does not demand. He serves. In his service the spiritual leader sets an example for the body- an example that has compelling power to motivate heart change" (115). There are other writers who agree with this idea, but the most poignant is Christ's ultimate modeling behavior mentioned in John 3:16. *"For God so loved the world that He gave His one and only Son, that whoever believes in Him shall not perish but have eternal life."* Jesus Christ embodies a selfless act in dying as an innocent Savior for a guilty world.

There is no greater sacrifice. While Christians are not necessarily called to die in the same way Christ died, Christians are called to heed His example of total selflessness, especially as leaders.

Leadership is membership in the body. Servant leaders are called together for the cause of Christ. Whether one's leadership is in a secular organization, non-profit or church, or any combination, each is a part of the body of Christ and must understand the systemic nature of this relationship. This calls for servant leaders to accept positions of leadership as a means to serve, to model the behavior of servant leadership, and build the bench strength of servant leadership for the future. In this brief study of the New Testament, it is apparent that servant leadership is different from secular leadership and management. In conclusion, it can be stated that servant leadership is not a leadership or management style. Servant leadership is a leadership worldview that works in conjunction with other leadership styles. One can be a military leader where consensus management is not the norm, but can be a servant to the group. One could employ an executive style of leadership or one that is more commanding and controlling, but still employ the principles of servant leadership.

Servant leaders are called to serve. Servant leaders can aspire to levels of authority, but only as a means of additional service. These leaders practice selflessness and assist others in becoming servants. No matter the position or the organization, a servant leader always places the needs of others over him/herself.

Studying the biblical theology of leadership provided the theological underpinnings for studying church leadership. Having this biblical view in place, the review pointed out that leadership and management principles are similar in most arenas of organizational leadership. Previous research was then reviewed to better understand related areas of ministerial effectiveness and the minister as manager. The literature related to the executive pastor revealed certain practices that are consistent in this position.

The review of pertinent literature has revealed that there is limited research on the new phenomenon of the executive pastor. Pertinent literature provided foundational support for the leadership and management functions necessary for the local church. Literature on servant leadership revealed that servant leadership is more of a leadership worldview than a type of leadership. Servant leadership was seen as necessary for leadership generally, but critical for the executive pastor. Certain competencies were reviewed as appropriate for leadership practice. This review of the literature revealed that certain critical competencies for church practice paralleled secular nonprofit and for-profit leadership competency research. These competencies were viewed as appropriate and applicable to the church context. Previous research on ministry practices revealed that there are certain competencies that are appropriate for the minister. Management and administration are functions necessary for ministry effectiveness.

From the pertinent literature, a listing of the stated practices was completed. The management and leadership construct provided by Alec Mackenzie provided the framework for analyzing this ministry position.

Chapter Five
Summary and Conclusions

Undertaking this study revealed much to me and demonstrates that I have been taken through the rebuilding and restructuring of a ministry. Many leadership techniques and skills were used for this research. One must remember that building a ministry is tough, painful, pressuring, humbling but rewarding. In this reference tool, I have spoken about personality traits of an unwise leader as well as a leader that is willing to take constructive criticism and willing to change. Ed Cole states: "Change is not change until its change."

As a leader, your team members change you in a certain way. You give them the vision and encourage them, and in turn, they give you what you have given them. If it was good impartation, you receive that back through their production and their day-to-day dealings with you as a leader. If you are always frustrated and negative, then your staff will produce frustrated and negative results, and your ministry will be frustrated as a whole.

Managers and leaders are very different kinds of people. They differ in motivation, personal history, and in how they think and act. Managers work in problem solving to coordinate and balance opposing views to reach consensus. Leaders work in the opposite direction. Where managers act to limit choices, leaders develop fresh approaches to long-standing problems and open issues to new options. To be effective, leaders must project their ideas onto images that excite people and only then develop choices that give those images substance.

Leaders tolerate chaos and lack of structure and are thus prepared to keep answers in suspense, avoiding premature closure on important issues. Managers seek order and control and are almost compulsively addicted to disposing of problems even before they understand their potential significance. Seldom do the uncertainties of potential chaos cause problems. Instead, it is the instinctive move to impose order on potential chaos that makes trouble for organizations.

References

Akuchie, Celestina N. Nov 11, 2014. *The Divine Chain.* Tate Publishing.

Bass, B. M. (1985). *Leadership and performance beyond expectation.* New York: Free Press.

Bennis, Warren. *On Becoming a Leader* 4th Edition. Mar 3, 2009. Basic Books.

Block, Peter and Steven Piersanti. May 20, 2013. *Stewardship: Choosing Service Over Self-Interest.* Berrett-Koehler Publishers

Brennan, Dennis. *As a Leader: 15 Points to Consider for More Inclusive Leadership.* Feb 11, 2014. Tate Publishing.

Brown, Tom and Ken Iverson. May 01, 1998. *Art of Keeping Management Simple: An Interview with Ken Iverson of Nucor Steel.* Harvard Business Review.

Byham, William and Jeff Cox. Jul 18, 1995. *Heroz: Empower Yourself, Your Coworkers, Your Company.* Ballantine Books.

Carlson, Marilyn. Sep 11, 2008. *How We Lead Matters: Reflections on a Life of Leadership.* Nelson McGraw-Hill Education.

Collins, Jim. Oct 16, 2001. *Good to Great: Why Some Companies Make the Leap and Others Don't.* HarperBusiness.

Covey, Stephen R. Nov 19, 2013. *The 7 Habits of Highly Effective People: Powerful Lessons in Personal Change.* Simon & Schuster.

Creech, R. Robert and Jim Herrington. Jun 17, 2016. *The Leader's Journey: Accepting the Call to Personal and Congregational Transformation.* CreateSpace Independent Publishing Platform.

DuBrin, Andrew J. Jan 1, 2015. *Leadership: Research Findings, Practice, and Skills* 8th Edition. Cengage Learning.

Fournies, Ferdinand. Jun 7, 2007. *Why Employees Don't Do What They're Supposed To and What You Can Do About It.* McGraw-Hill Education.

Gangel, Kenneth O. Aug 1, 2000. *Feeding & Leading: Practical Handbook on Administration in Churches and Christian Organizations.* Baker Books.

Geneen, Harold and Brent Bowers. Apr 1997. *The Synergy Myth: And Other Ailments of Business Today.* St. Martin's Press.

Greenleaf, Robert K. Sep 30, 2015. *The Servant as Leader.* The Greenleaf Center for Servant Leadership.

Handy, Charles. September 1, 2000. *Twenty-One Ideas for Managers: Practical Wisdom for Managing Your Company and Yourself.* Jossey-Bass.

Harari, Oren. Aug 8, 2003. *The Leadership Secrets of Colin Powell.* McGraw-Hill Education.

Hartman, Taylor Ph.D. 1987. *The Color Code Paperback.*

Hildebrand, Kenneth. Import, 1957. *Finding Real Happiness Hardcover.* Arthur James.

Jay, Anthony. Jun 17, 1996. *MANAGEMENT & MACHIAVELLI: A Prescription for Success in Your Business.* Prentice Hall Press.

Katz, Daniel and Robert L. Kahn. Apr 24, 1978. *The Social Psychology of Organizations.* Wiley.

Katzenbach, Jon R. and Douglas K. Smith. Oct 13, 2015. *The Wisdom of Teams: Creating the High-Performance Organization.* Harvard Business Review Press.

Keith, Dr. Kent M. 1968 2001. *Anyway: The Paradoxical Commandments.* Putnam.

Korn/Ferry. 2009. *Leadership Architect Factor/Cluster Sort Card Deck.* Korn/Ferry International.

Kouzes, James M. and Barry Z. Posner. May 2, 2016. *Learning Leadership: The Five Fundamentals of Becoming an Exemplary Leader.* Wiley

MacKenzie, Alec. Jun 1991. *Managing Your Goals.* Nightingale Conant Corp

Maguire, Francis X. and Steve Williford. May 6, 2001. *You're the Greatest: How Validated Employees Can Impact Your Bottom Line.* Williford Communications.

Marriott, J.W. "Bill" Jr. May 5, 2014. *Without Reservations: How a Family Root Beer Stand Grew into a Global Hotel Company.* Luxury Custom Publishing.

Maxwell, John C. 1803. *Developing the Leaders Around You.* Thomas Nelson Inc.

Miller, William R. and Stephen Rollnick. Sep 7, 2012. *Motivational Interviewing: Helping People Change, 3rd Edition (Applications of Motivational Interviewing).* The Guilford Press.

Nouwen, Henri J.M. 1647. *In the Name of Jesus by Henri J.M. Nouwen.* Darton, Longman & Todd Ltd.

Peter, Dr. Laurence J. 1972. *The Peter Principle.* Bantam.

Peters, Thomas J. and Waterman, Robert H. Jr. Feb 7, 2006. *In Search of Excellence: Lessons from America's Best-Run Companies.* HarperBusiness

Peters, Tom. August 2, 1991. *Thriving on Chaos: Handbook for a Management Revolution.* Harper Perennial.

Piper, John. Feb 1, 2013. *Brothers, We Are Not Professionals: A Plea to Pastors for Radical Ministry, Updated and Expanded Edition.* B&H Books.

Richards, Lawrence O. and Clyde Hoeldtke. January 1, 1980 *A Theology Of Church Leadership.* Zondervan Publishing Company.

Secretan, Lance. Jun 6, 1994. *Managerial Moxie: The 8 Proven Steps to Empowering Employees and Supercharging Your Company.* Prima Lifestyles.

Secretan, Lance. Jun 2003. *Inspirational Leadership: Destiny, Calling & Cause.* Lance Secretan Publishing.

Spears, Larry C. May 29, 1995. *Reflections on Leadership: How Robert K. Greenleaf's Theory of Servant-Leadership Influenced Today's Top Management Thinkers.* Wiley.

Stayer, James A. and Ralph C. Belasco. August 1, 1994. *Flight of the Buffalo.* Grand Central Publishing.

U.S. Office of Personnel Management. *Leadership Assessment Program (LAP).* Federal Relay Service.

Walton, Mary and W. Edwards Deming. Nov 1, 1988. *The Deming Management Method.* Perigee Books

Weiss, Donald H. May 11, 1998. *Secrets of the Wild Goose: The Self-Management Way to Increase Your Personal Power and Inspire Productive Teamwork.* AMACOM

Wilkins, Robert H. May 1994. *The Quality-Empowered Business.* Prentice Hall Trade.

About the Author

Dr. Willie Holmes is a born leader. At the age of eighteen, he began to expand his ministry by hosting revivals in Chicago.

Dr. Holmes is dedicated to cultivating and enhancing new and established ministries of all forms. He is a destiny builder, sharpening leaders to meet their spiritual, emotional and social needs, through shaping themselves first to be Wise Builders. He has received many community awards for his unselfish acts of love in the community.

In 1996, Dr. Willie Holmes received his master's degree in Ministry and has worked hard to continue his education.
In 2000, he received his doctorate degree in Ministry. In July 2005-2006, Dr. Holmes was inducted into the Who's Who of America for his outstanding accomplishments

Dr. Holmes is in demand as one of the most dynamic speakers in America today. More than 8000 audiences in ten countries have attended his crusades and seminars.

Dr. Willie Holmes is a facilitator, author, and minister, life coach, song writer and entrepreneur. He is the founder and CEO of Global Non-Denominational Assemblies.

Furthermore, he is a husband and a father of five children.